ARE WE WE FREE NOW MOMMA?

1877
Presents

The Crow Code 1877

E.J. Wade

TABLE OF CONTENTS

The CC 1877

RLFJC

ACT 1

1863

(A young man runs down the hall as fast as he can. He runs past the secretary who tries to stop him. He enters a room and hands a letter to an older man who puts on his glasses to read it.)

William: Boy do you know what this is?

Johnny: No Sir

William: President Lincoln just Emancipated 3 and a half million Negro men, women, and children.

Johnny: That's good right?

William stands up and removes his glasses. He starts to cry as Johnny and the secretary stares at him. William had participated in a long fight on the side of the Radical Republicans for this victory. (scene)

A group of men gather in a room to discuss the Emancipation and what the next steps should be.

William: President Lincoln is only asking for 10 percent loyalty in order to accept these traitors back into the union!

This is preposterous! Benjamin Wade of Ohio and Henry Davis of Maryland are calling for 100 percent loyalty to the Union. We want an ironclad allegiance. We can't allow traitors to rejoin with amnesty.

Robert: The president is more concerned with putting The Union back together.

William: My dear friend, what is a union without freedom? To say you will accept 10 percent loyalty is to say you will allow 90 percent disloyalty. The same disloyalty that almost destroyed our great nation. We have fought too hard and too long. I knew Lincoln would try to make friends with rebels.

Robert: The ranking members will be dealt with. We can't punish thousands of men. Thomas, have faith good sir.

William: If the president allows this to happen, he will rue the day! The spirit of rebellion is at hand. He has to crush the enemy now and also free the other half a million Negro men, women, and children!

Robert: The president can only use his rights as Commander -in-Chief. He can only go after the work force of the rebel states. The states that have succeeded from the Union. The poor going off to die for the wealthy. The war could have been avoided.

William: I will never forgive the rest of the Republicans if they don't help us persuade the President. (scene)

(Both chambers of congress, now dominated by Republicans successfully pass the Wade-Davis Bill in - 1864. President Lincoln decides to pocket –veto the bill and allow the congressional session to end without signing it into law. Lincoln receives some push back but wins reelection with Andrew Johnson as his running mate. Andrew Johnson was a Democrat.)

1865

Ford's Theatre, Washington D.C.

(President Lincoln is enjoying himself with family friends when Actor John Wilkes Booth shoots the president behind the ear killing him. President Lincoln was able to pass the 13th Amendment but was assassinated before it was ratified in all states)

(Robert arrives at the home of Thomas and knocks 3 times on the door, Thomas gives Robert a hard stare and then takes a seat.)

Thomas: I am waiting for William to grace us with his presence. Would you like some apple pie? I'll have my grandson fetch us some pie and tea. The president is a fighter. We now have the 13th Amendment to the constitution because of him. I know William will be pleased. President Lincoln may have blocked the Wade-Davis bill but perhaps he is on the side of freedom.

Robert: Thomas, the president was shot.

(Thomas looks up at Robert with pain in his eyes).

Thomas: No, that can't be…

(Martha overheard the two men and walked into the dining room. She starts to cry as Thomas gets up to console her.)

Thomas: We have to get William now!

(The two men travel to the home of William who did not show for the meeting. William had already heard the news of the Presidents death.)

Thomas: William!

William: You came bearing bad news? I know, the no good dogs have killed our president. I don't care anymore! God Damn it all! If congress does not stop them I will run for a seat myself.

Thomas: We need your leadership right now. Mobs are attacking Democrats. People have gone mad!

William: Let the mobs have those traitors! I told you all! Treason I tell you! Treason! I say we hang them all by the necks. A reckoning. Do you know what your problem is? You worry about the color of the new Union. I worry about the character. Thaddeus was right, too many whites have a broken moral compass.

Robert: Vice President Andrew Johnson was sworn in today.

William: What is to become of the 3 and a half million Negro men, women, and children? We all know President Johnson is not a friend of the Negro. Today is truly a sad day as providence looks down upon us.

Thomas: Can we count on your leadership? William, the future of the Republican Party is now at stake. Give me that whiskey!

William: Perhaps the decision to make a pro slavery

Democrat his vice president was short sided. Leave my whiskey alone. Do you know what you are Thomas? You are a coward, you kiss rebel tail. You all will have to answer to God.

Thomas: You have never had faith in our President or our party William! Don't you "frog up on me". You stand with us. The fight has just begun. My brother's will you stand with me?

William: What are we going to do now?

Thomas: We pass the Civil Rights Act and then we quickly go for a 14th Amendment.

William: The Negro men must be allowed to vote. The South will be rebuilt by Negro men and white men alike. I also would like to confiscate the land from the slavers and give it to the workers. We make all Americans the same. No white and no black, just American.

Thomas: Let us go and gather the rest of the Republicans. We have much work to do. The freedmen and women need us. More importantly, the Union needs us. William, we need you to stop at the edge. You can't be too radical. The situation is delicate.

William: Do you know what too radical is? Taking human beings, reducing them to animals, and pretending God has something to do with it. That is radical, I am logical. The bastards should see how it feels to have a government take everything from you.

(A man enters the room. He is older and needs assistance with moving around. The gentleman removes his hat)

William: Thaddeus!

1866

Thaddeus Stevens Speaks to Clay Swanson in a conference room

Thaddeus Stevens: I fought tooth and nail to push President Lincoln towards freeing the enslaved men, women, and children who have suffered for far too long. Now President Johnson wants to take us backwards. Those men who died on the battlefield did not die in vain! We will not give the country back to the Devil.

Clay: The Emancipation Proclamation was an overreach. A tyrant president who takes the property of rebels and then claims niggers aren't property. Now you seek to make a federal law! The Yankees keep putting their foot on our necks. The niggers are our economy you foolish dog.

Thaddeus Stevens: I have always wanted complete freedom. I tolerated President Lincoln but you sir are no President and Johnson became President only because of a lousy bullet. The Civil Rights Act is needed to give guidance and prevent white people's inner compass from going in the wrong way as it usually does.

Clay: President Johnson said we can govern our own affairs. You want animals to be able to make contracts and sue good white Christians in court. If congress passes this law we will get President Johnson to make it disappear. I am tired of your self-pity Thaddeus. Perhaps you want to be a nigger.

Thaddeus Stevens: We will be more than happy to go after President Johnson. You want a fight, I still have fight left in me. I received the news that whites have been burning down the Negro homes and shooting them as they run out in New Orleans.

Clay: The disloyal animals should die. I'll kill them all myself if I can!

(Thaddeus Stevens storms out of the room)

William: Thaddeus, What is wrong?

Thaddeus Stevens: Congress is about to be back in session. I want Andrew "empty headed" Johnson impeached and we will bring federal troops down into the south.

William: I thought you would never pull the trigger my dear friend. Freedom for all people!

Thaddeus Stevens: If we don't kill the Devil now he will rewrite history and undo what we have done!

(Federal Troops arrive in the South to protect newly freed black people from racial terrorism from white mobs)

The Civil Rights Act of 1866 has passed by a two-thirds vote.
Negro men and women gather in South Carolina. 1868

(The group gathers at the small but fancy community hall. As soon as blacks were emancipated they started generating a middle and upper class. Many were still working poor but tales traveled throughout the country of the success stories.)

Deacon Senior: Thank you for coming everyone. I have good news! The Lord Jesus has swung his mighty sword from the heavens! On July 9, 1868 the 14th Amendment to the constitution was ratified throughout the union.

Unknown woman: What it mean Senior?

Deacon Senior: It means Negroes are now equal to whites and the government will protect our rights as humans. The Civil Rights Act and the 14th Amendment means we have weapons to fight back against these black codes that are coming about. We also have troops to protect us from the angry mobs.

(Cheers from the crowd)

Deacon Senior: Wait, now for the bad news. Thaddeus Stevens also has passed away and went to be with our lord. It says he died on August 11th. We will pray for his family.

Abbie: My daddy met Thaddeus Stevens before. He was a good man! Tonight we enjoy not only freedom but we gone be equal!

(Cheers from the crowd)

Deacon Senior: My little girl. What a woman you have become. You gone make a fine wife. My grand babies will be born equal. We finally won. The Negro is finally part of America.

Abbie: Tonight we eat and we don't worry. Wait here, I'm going to bring you some food.

Moses: While Abbie is gone I wanted to ask for permission to court your little girl sir.

Deacon Senior: God be the glory. You're going to have your own church someday. I have always been fond of you Moses. I love you like a son. Go say hi to Abbie. Go on now, don't be shy boy.

(Moses gathers himself and walks over to Abbie)

Moses: Senior Deacon, I mean Deacon Senior wanted us to talk.

Abbie: My daddy is up to his old tricks. Well I'm going to Fisk University. Negroes just got free and we already building our own schools and businesses and even churches. I don't want to settle down yet.

Moses: Abbie, you already 20. You a good age to be a momma. I was thinking we can have our own church. You want to leave Carolina?

Abbie: I want to be a smart woman with a life to live. My own life, not Mr. old Deacon Senior

(Abbie mocks her father's deep voice)

Moses: What if I make a church near Fisk?

(Abbie throws her arms up and walks away)

Abbie: Momma, how come men don't understand women?

Mable: That is an Ancient question my dear child. The world is yours now, still young and full of life. Your daddy will be fine.

Abbie: What made you choose daddy?

Mable: He was brave enough to ask old masa Sullivan to let us jump the broom.

Abbie: Did Masa Sullivan touch you Mamma?

(Silence)

Mable: I never forgave myself.

Abbie: You didn't do nothing wrong.

Mable: He had me before your father

Abbie: You're safe now Mama. If any man touches you I'll kill them.

Mable: Listen to you…

In 1869 Ulysses S. Grant becomes President of a full Union

William: With Ulysses Grant as President perhaps we can finally get the Klan out of our hair and put this fight to rest. I have grown tired and weary and Thaddeus is no longer with us. President Johnson slowed us down but perhaps we can enjoy real reconstruction.

Thomas: Congratulations William. I know you have been fighting alongside the Republicans to make all of this happen. It is time to turn our watch over to younger people perhaps. The14th Amendment will stand forever. Those Democrats can never kill it.

Robert: I will take my rest somewhere other than Washington. There's something about Washington that always makes my skin crawl.

William: Perhaps lying down with Democrat dogs. Forgive me.

Robert: What is to become of the Negro now?

William: If whites stay out of there way they will flourish just fine.

Robert: William, you did a good thing. You helped a truly noble cause.

South Carolina:

Theo Wade: Mercy (whispers) Hey Mercy…

Mercy Justice peeks from behind a building and looks over at Theo Wade. He points to a house about a quarter mile away. The two men run to the house. Theo Wade knocks hard on the door and hides. An older man comes to the door.

BIG GUS: Who goes there?

Mercy Justice: I am looking for MJ Senior. He was sold to your plantation from down the road.

BIG GUS: I don't know no MJ boy. Get your black ass…

(Mercy points a gun at the white man)

BIG GUS: Do you know who I am boy!

Mercy Justice: Theo have a look around.

(Theo Wade looks around the home and the former slave quarters. He calls MJ's name a few times. A young boy pops up out of nowhere.)

MJ Senior: My name use to be MJ Senior.

Theo Wade: What do you mean use to be…

MJ Senior: Masa say my name Beau now

Theo Wade: Come here boy!

BIG GUS: Hey! Hey!

Mercy Justice: Sir, if you move again, I will blow your head off!

BIG GUS: I own a contract for an apprenticeship for that nigger boy.

Mercy Justice: run!

(Theo Nods his head. The three take off running.)

BIG GUS: You God damned Niggers!

(The homeowner reaches for a rifle and gives chase, he fires a shot but misses)

Theo Wade: He is running after us Mercy!

(Mercy turns around and takes aim at the homeowner, he fires a shot and drops the homeowner to the ground. He turns to catch up with the other two)

(Deacon Senior waits and paces back and forth as he waits patiently for Mercy Justice to return)

Deacon Senior: You hard headed boy! What have you done?

Mercy Justice: I got your boy back. Now pay up old man. A deal is a deal.

Deacon Senior: You fool, you risk our democracy for money

Mercy Justice: I don't have young ins but if I did no white man would ever take them. You hired me to do what you were scared to do yourself. Pay me my money. If a Justice of the Peace shows up I'll deal with them.

Deacon Senior: You think you're better than the law.

Mercy Justice: I am just as rotten as the white man but you need me. You need people like me to pull the trigger so that Negroes like you can walk around with your fancy clothes.

Deacon Senior: May Jesus touch your soul sir.

Mercy Justice: I don't know no Jesus and I don't want to know no Jesus sir.

Deacon Senior: Take your money and go boy.

1870

Robert E. Lee Dies 15th Amendment is ratified

Gus: Not too long ago, a nigger killed my papi and stole his apprentice. My Papi had bad hands and could not do the work for himself. The northern aggression against our States rights has to end. Robert E. Lee was like God to me. South Carolina now is governed by crooked nigger politicians. They steal and steal some more. Today we say no more.

Paul: I disagree. The mostly Negro congress have established education and allow whites to have our own schools as well. They do not force us to go to school with the Negro children.

Gus: Allow! Allow! Niggers don't allow us to do anything. How can someone who was born of lower intelligence allow me to do anything?

Paul: We can just live separately from the Negro. We can live in peace and just work together. We don't have to like them. Gus we have to tell the truth to each other. It's not really about them being dumb. If we have to pass a law outlawing reading then that means we know they are capable of reading. We need to tell the truth to ourselves in order to win this battle. Sell the idea of a danger.

Gus: I'll give you truth. First they made us free our slaves. Then they let the niggers vote and now they run the government. Next, they will pass laws saying we have to surrender our white daughters to the nigger men. Are you ready to give your little girl to one of them?

Paul: Yes, that is the truth. It will scare the nation because it scares me too. The Republicans will go too far and they will give Negroes our women, and our daughters. That will be the sword of truth that we shall fight with.

Rufus: What about the women?

Gus: She makes babies doesn't she? You have to kill the whole race. You can't spare women. The next thing you know, one of you stupid Peckerwoods will give the women a baby and it will be black which defeats the whole damn purpose of killing all the men!

Paul: Perhaps we should table this discussion. We can still make peace.

Gus: Peace? They're letting them build schools. Don't say I didn't warn you.

1872

Ulysses S. Grant Wins Re-election
1875

(Voices only! Republicans and Democrats battle over a New Civil Rights Bill)

Alexander Stephens: The Civil Rights bill of 1875 is unconstitutional. This goes beyond States rights and it violates the rights of citizens. How can you make whites sit next to Negroes on public transportation or allow Negroes to just be around white folks whenever they please? What if that white citizen does not want to be around the Negro? You can't use the law to make people like the Negro! They are trying to solve social issues with the Federal Government. We can surely find a better way to spend our time.

Robert Brown Elliott: I recall having to travel and not being able to stay in a Hotel. We pay taxes and these businesses benefit from my taxes. Senator Stephens being the former Vice President of the Confederacy enjoys rights. The rights of my entire race is at stake. We should enjoy the same rights of our former oppressors.

United States V. Cruikshank
92 U.S. 542 1876
William gets the bad news

Martha: Robert Brown Elliott rebutted Alexander Stephens and he was so brilliant. William you would have been proud. A beautiful and intelligent Negro man stood before congress and showed the nation that our mission was not in vain! The Civil Rights Act of 1875 had plenty of support!

William: Thank you Martha, I know you don't like me reading up on politics now. My old heart can't take bad news. What a day that must have been…

Martha: I also have to tell you United States V. Cruikshank did not go our way.

William: They are setting a precedent for white citizens to just be able to attack Negroes whenever they please. Over 100 Freedmen murdered in Colfax, most of them surrendered and the cowards shot them dead anyway. It's like the Supreme Court is taking part in the killing. If local law refuses to do anything and then courts join in on the murder what other options do they have?

Martha: The White League and the Red Shirts!

William: They pulled the trigger but the government allowed this. Now the Freedmen have to worry about getting shot for trying to vote with no protection. This kills the Enforcement Act of 1870. The majority of the judges are Republican appointees by Lincoln and Grant. Something does not sit well with me. Something is terribly wrong.

Tilden or Blood

Gus: Are the votes in yet?

Paul: No, not yet but it is dangerously close

Gus: Tilden is our Democrat. He will make sure the Nigger is no longer the favorite.

Paul: The favorite?

Gus: You heard me loud and clear sir. The niggers have become the government's favorite. I saw a nigger playing the piano. I can't play no piano. I ain't got no fancy clothes. I see dark women and men in fancy clothes. They are uppity now, looking white Christians in the eye. The Civil Rights Act of 1875. I told you they would try to force us to love niggers. They're coming for our women. I told you Paul.

(Rufus enters the room)

Rufus: The election is still deadlocked. Rutherford B. Hayes and Republicans are trying to steal this election.

Gus: Do you see what I mean? The crooked Republicans and their animals. I won't watch them steal another election. Gather the men and send the boy to fetch Badger.

Paul: No, please don't get Badger.

Gus: It is time, Grateful Gus is over. I will help the rest of these southern gentleman restore order. Send for Badger now!

The Electoral Commission of 1876.

Joseph P. Bradley: Gentleman thank you for choosing me as the final member. A total of 15 members. 5 from the Democrat controlled House of Representatives. 5 Members of the Republican controlled Senate and 5 members of the Supreme Court. We have gathered to decide who will be the next President of the United States and deal with the Negro problem.

Voice: Roll Call

Josiah Abbott, Massachusetts/ Samuel Miller, Iowa/

Thomas Bayard, Delaware/ Oliver Morton, Indiana/

Joseph Bradley, New Jersey/ Henry Pain, Ohio/

Nathan Clifford, Maine/ William Strong, Pennsylvania/

George F. Edmunds, Vermont/ Allen Thurman, Ohio/

Stephen Field, California/

Frederick Frelinghuysen, New Jersey

James Garfield, Ohio

George Hoar, Massachusetts

Eppa Hunton,Virginia

(gavel)

Paul: According to Mr. Chandler's numbers the contested states are enough to literally hand the race to Hayes!

Lyman Trumbull: I am in the corner of Tilden. I think the end slavery was a good idea. Free Negro labor hurts the white man and I believe the Republican Party is the white man's party. There are 20 electoral votes being contested. Does anyone in this room wish to speak? This is official but unofficial.

Paul: I'm sorry you represent Tilden? Are you currently Republican or Democrat?

Lyman Trumbull: I have been on both sides if that is what you are hinting at. In a few hours none of that will matter sir.

Paul: You helped write the 13th Amendment but you helped Andrew Johnson escape impeachment. I was curious.

William Strong: The Democrats are asking for a railroad to help support and sustain an economy since you took away our property. We can bring around Florida, Louisiana, and South Carolina.

Lyman Trumbull: What Mr. … I'm sorry what is your name?

Paul: Just call me Paul.

Lyman Trumbull: Paul, You are focused on the wrong colors. Red and Blue will no longer matter after this. White is the only color that matters.

William Strong: I fully agree. I am Democrat and I am Republican. The white man owns them both.

Paul: I see your vision. The problem is we have people who need more than a railroad.

William Strong: Why don't you just bring us your boss?

(Badger enters the room)

Badger: I thought you would never ask.

Lyman Trumbull: What are the people asking for?

Badger: A presidential election is important. The only thing more important than the white house is to make sure it remains a white house. You need to maintain our southern way of life. We don't want any more northern interference.

Paul: That sounds like a good idea.

Lyman Trumbull: I am already onboard with States rights.

Badger: We need a new economy and we need the rest of the Federal Troops removed so that we can deal with our traitor niggers.

Paul: Wait… what?

Badger: The federal government will look the other way while we deal with those traitors. Running to another state to fight their masters. We can't forgive that. We are going to put those niggers back in their place. At the bottom of my shoes.

Paul: They're citizens now, with equal protection under the law. The constitution…

Badger: What constitution? I don't see any constitution, at lease when it comes to them.

Lyman Trumbull: How do you suppose we go around the constitution sir?

Badger: We have Supreme Court justices and both parties right here. If we all agree and we have unity then we will simply ignore the law. If I go home and have a lynch party…

Paul: They will go to the law

Badger: Look around, we are the law.

Paul: I was on board with the plan but this is more treason. Is there a way to come together without being criminals?

Lyman Trumbull: Perhaps it's not the federal government's job to hold the Negroes hand. We gave them approximately 10 years to get their act together. What's taking so long?

Paul: They were slaves for hundreds of years. They are already building Colleges.

Lyman Trumbull: We gave them special attention. I think we have done our job. We brought them to America and made them Christian.

Badger: Gus told me you were getting a little soft on them. Think about it this way, our motivations are different. I want my Grandkids to look like my Grandparents and if that means killing them all, I will kill them all and any whites who get in the way. We can do "Tilden or Blood" and hurt some folks or maybe Hayes wins and we only kill the dark skinned traitors. What we couldn't win in war we will win in peace and what didn't kill us only made us stronger. The south will rise again.

Lyman Trumbull: A railroad, economy, troop removal and freedom to do with the Negro as you please. Tilden loses but we maintain dignity.

Badger: You can even say Rutherford B. Hayes stole the election. We can pretend to hate each other, Republicans versus Democrats but we know the truth. It will always be white over black.

Paul: White over black

Lyman Trumbull: To States Rights!

William Strong: Forever, white over black

(The room full of men begin to shake hands and say "white over black".)

1877

South Carolina:

(Mercy spots Abbie going out to get some water)

Mercy Justice: Excuse me ma'am. I couldn't help but notice your beauty. You look like the sky and the stars gave birth to you.

Abbie: You slick tongue devil. What brings you to our little part of town?

Mercy Justice: I came back to check on MJ Senior.

Abbie: What do you want with my little brother?

Mercy Justice: You're Deacon Seniors kin?

Abbie: Yes, I am his daughter. Come say hi.

Mercy Justice: I better not ma'am

Abbie: Come on you big baby.

(The two approach the church)

Deacon Senior: Well, The sinner has returned

Mercy Justice: Good evening sir, perhaps we got off on

the wrong foot.

Abbie: Daddy he knows MJ.

Deacon Senior: I know why you here. You got eyes for my little girl. You not yoked the same. She needs a Christian man.

Abbie: I'm going to Fisk. This is my life daddy.

Mercy Justice: I actually discovered Jesus since we last met sir.

Deacon Senior: Is that so?

Mercy Justice: Yes Sir

Deacon Senior: Did you get baptized son?

Mercy Justice: What?

(Scene cuts to Deacon Senior and Moses dipping Mercy Justice in the water)

Mercy Justice: This water cold sir! Wait!

Deacon Senior: Get your ass in that water

(dips Justice in the water)

Mercy Justice: Too much water

Deacon Senior: Boy you got a dirty soul you need to stay in longer

(dips Justice back into the water)

Abbie: Daddy stop!

Deacon Senior: We gone get all that sin and lust out you boy!

(Mercy runs out of the water as fast as he can, Deacon and Moses laugh)

Abbie: You can be a real hypocrite sometimes Daddy. That's not funny!

Deacon Senior: You will never marry my little girl!

Abbie: Mercy I'm sorry.

Mercy Justice: I'm fine. You folks enjoy your day.

(Mercy walks off angry as Moses and Deacon Senior smirk)

(Mable approaches)

Mable: Deacon, we have a new president. Rutherford B. Hayes won.

Washington

William: Thomas, Robert, come in. It has been too long since the last time we had a chat.

Thomas: How have you been old friend?

William: Well look at me

Robert: Still the most ugly son of a bitch on this side of the planet

William: Go to hell Robert. How can I help you guys?

Thomas: The Republicans have the White House.

William: At what cost?

Thomas: The troops will be removed immediately and the Federal government will allow the South the freedom to deal with the Negro themselves. They have also been given approval for a railroad and help building a new economy.

William: What does that mean? A new economy for who?

Robert: I'm sorry William

William: We must gather the remaining radical Republicans at once. We have to make sure the rights we secured for all Americans are safe.

Robert: We are finished William. We have to focus on building an economy. The Negro will be fine. They have manage to do a lot in a few years. I can only imagine what they will do in 100.

William: I will gather the men myself!

Thomas: You're out William!

William: You traitors! You got your 30 pieces of silver didn't you?

Thomas: William, they will be fine.

William: Our democracy is fragile. You know we have thousands of angry rebels ready to seek revenge on Negro people for wanting to be free. What are they supposed to do?

Thomas: I am truly sorry. We will continue to be the party of all Americans.

William: Their blood will be on your hands! How dare you! The presidency of Rutherford B. Hayes is not worth the lives of millions of freedmen who now depend on the union for protection. You gave up the freedom of an entire race for one lousy president!

Robert: Does whites fighting whites seem right to you? Why is it the Unions job to protect them?

William: Do you think Negroes chose this fight? Do you think they had a choice Robert?

Robert: We have to go now. Enjoy your rest. I am truly sorry my friend.

William: Don't you walk away from me! Hey! Hey! I hope you traitor's burn in hell! You have blood on your hands! Do you hear me! We still have time Robert. Don't turn your back on millions of people.

(Robert and Thomas walk away. Robert wipes a tear from his eye)

Robert: How do you feel Thomas?

Thomas: At lease we helped abolish slavery. That should be enough. I don't want to have to look over my shoulder every day. The union is together and even if Negroes can't be a full part of it at lease they are not slaves.

South Carolina

Abbie: Are you heading back west Mr. Justice?

Mercy Justice: Yes, we just got news that Hayes won the election and they are about to withdraw federal troops from the South. You guys should be real careful now. Ain't no telling what they got planned for us now.

Deacon Senior: I'm sure we will be just fine. If something happens we can provide safety at the church.

Mable: Make sure you're safe travelling on that road Mr. Justice.

Mercy Justice: Yes Ma'am.

(Deacon Senior starts to close his church when he sees troops leaving on their horses.)

Mable: Maybe things will be fine.

Deacon Senior: They gave us from 1866 until now. That's 11 years to repair hundreds of years of slavery. The same black codes Andrew Jackson allowed are about to return. I hate to say this Mable but we need guns.

Mable: You know how I feel about guns Senior.

Deacon Senior: Honey, the troops are leaving. Them crackers about to start drinking and getting themselves into a tizzy, they gonna start attacking.

(Deacon Senior starts gathering wood when a drunk man approaches Isabella, one of their church members.)

Rufus: Hey girl! Hey. You got some Spaniard in you.

How would you like to be with a real man?

Isabella: You seem drunk sir!

Rufus: Good, that's how I like it.

Deacon Senior: Sir, we don't want no trouble.

Rufus: I wasn't talking to you boy. Look down when you talk to me. This is the white man's country again.

Deacon Senior: Sir, please leave.

Rufus: Are you giving me orders boy?

Deacon Senior: Like I said sir… the last thing I want is trouble.

Rufus: Well you got trouble coming to you nigger. I'm coming back.

(Rufus rides off)

Isabella: Maybe we should leave.

Deacon Senior: We supposed to leave and go where? I know people left to go north and they poor. We built something and we won't be run off.

(Mable hugs Isabella)

(Meanwhile Rufus meets with his people down the road)

Rufus: That uppity nigger told me I better never show my face again.

Gus: Is that what he really said?

Rufus: Are you calling me a lie Gus?

Paul: Everything is going to be fine.

Gus: Paul, you get a message to the old Deacon. Tell him he has until Badger arrives to leave the state. Badger is coming and he got some real Klan members. He gone be the first to hang.

(Paul leaves to warn Deacon Senior)

Holly Springs, Mississippi

(Badger walks out of a store and looks around. He sees a young lady hand some candy to a kid. He approaches.)

Badger: You all didn't steal that candy did you?

Ida B. Wells: No, we didn't

Badger: Well what's your name young lady?

Ida B. Wells: My name is Ida Wells sir.

Badger: Ida Wells. Why don't you go on home. Gone now, get!

(The young girl looks at Badger but doesn't flinch. He laughs and walks away)

South Carolina

(Rufus returns to the church with help.)

Rufus: Mr. uppity deacon over here wants some trouble.

Deacon Senior: Sir, I just want to keep the peace. We won't bother you, we good Christian folks.

Rufus: Yea, we good Christian folks too, not the same kind of Christian as you boy.

Deacon Senior: Only one Jesus Christ Sir.

Rufus: He won't save your kind.

Deacon Senior: Sir, I think you should leave and stay gone this time.

(Rufus spits on the ground)

Paul: Deacon, things are about to get a lot worse for you and your people. The Republicans won't protect your kind anymore.

Isabella: We got rights! I am a visitor from another country, you treat people bad.

Rufus: Huh uh nigger, or should I say half nigger. Your rights are over.

Deacon Senior: The 14th amendment has been ratified sir. It says "No state shall make or enforce any law which shall abridge the privileges …

Rufus: Who taught you how to read?

Paul: Listen, I don't fully agree with going back to the old way of how things were done but that day has come. You have until Badger arrives to leave or we will come see you.

(The men ride away)

Mable: I think we should all leave.

Deacon Senior: No, just the women and children. The men will stay and fight.

Mable: Even if you get a gun, you ain't got enough bullets for all them crackers Senior.

Deacon Senior: I'm going to gather some men. I'll be with Moses.

(Mable, Isabella, and Abbie pack up for a trip and decide to head out, while heading out of town they are stopped by a white mob. They begin to circle the women with their horses)

White League Member 1: Why are you riding near white property?

Mable: We are leaving for good sir, we don't want no trouble.

White League Member 1: Well, you got trouble. We are going to let you go, but the Spaniard is mine.

(White League member 2 reaches for Isabella, Abbie quickly draws a gun)

Abbie: You keep your dirty hands off of her.

(The men laugh)

White League Member 1: We will be on our way.

White League Member 2: We will meet again

Abbie: I will save some bullets

(The men ride off, the women try to comfort Isabella as she cries)

(Badger finally arrives in South Carolina, he looks around as whites and blacks walk around doing business and working.)

Badger: Sitting around in fancy clothes. Reading the constitution and playing piano. Well, South Carolina belongs to the white man. There won't be any more piano playing. I think it's time to get some traitors and hang them from a tree. (Scene)

(Isabella, Mable, and Abbie make a stop the next town over, they get some rough looks as they stop to look after their horses)

Abbie: I don't feel right about leaving father behind.

Mable: We can't go back.

Abbie: Maybe you guys can head further north and I will head back.

Mable: Please spend the night with us. If you must head back do it in the morning.

Abbie: I am sorry, I have to ride under the cover of night.

(Abbie heads back towards town to help her father while Mable and Isabella stay in a lodge for Negroes)

The End of Act 1

ACT 2

(A letter from William)

Dear brothers,

By the time you read this letter, I am certain I will no longer be on this Earth. I am honored to say that I have stood in the company of true Sons of God. Men who did everything in our power to break the evil chains of slavery versus men who kill to establish racial hierarchy. The Negro, who they refer to as savage, wanted freedom for all and walked away peacefully after hundreds of years of slavery. It was us, the white men who decided freedom should never be an option if your skin is dark. I stand ashamed of our hypocrisy. We claimed to have left Europe to establish freedom and then we instead took it. God's judgement sits upon our great nation. The reckoning of the Civil War will be 10 times worse. The evil spirit only waits for its final destination. Remember us for the good. Remember us for the freedom and the fight! We didn't lose, our way it will just take longer than we thought. The stone that the builder refused will always be the corner stone. The people who built this nation will rise again. It won't be today or tomorrow. There will be a great lion and that lion will divide itself by three. The three will honor their ancestors and the ancestors will lend them the power to ultimately destroy white supremacy. The free will rise again.

William Monroe

(Mercy Justice was informed about the end of reconstruction and the new world to come under President Rutherford B. Hayes. He decided to head back south to check up on Abbie. Mercy usually travelled with his close friend Theo Wade. Due to the rise of black citizens being attacked Mercy headed back with a group of men. Mercy, Thomas, Ben, Eugene, Leonard, Virgil, and Theo. The group of men enter South Carolina through Native American territory)

Mercy Justice: Eugene, do you know which tribe occupies this area?

Eugene: Give me time to think

Mercy Justice: I thought you said you know this area? Were they slave owners?

Eugene: Yes, they owned slaves.

Mercy Justice: Get off the horses. Blow out the light.

Theo Wade: How do we get through here with no light?

Mercy Justice: Everybody get behind me. Form a line. I'm going to whisper, the person behind me will whisper and we will follow each other's voice down the line. Hey, follow the person in front of you, wait for the sound of their voice.

(The men creep silently through the territory)

Mercy Justice: Get low, get low brother

Eugene: Get low, get low brother

Theo Wade: Get low, get low brother

Leonard: Get low, get low brother

Virgil: Get low, get low brother

Ben: Get low, get low brother

Thomas: Get low, get low brother

Mercy Justice: Get low, get low brother

Eugene: Get low, get low brother

Theo Wade: Get low, get low brother

Leonard: Get low, get low brother

Virgil: Get low, get low brother

Ben: Get low, get low brother

Thomas: Get low, get low brother

(The men keep repeating as they creep through the territory. One of the horses is startled and starts to make noise)

Mercy Justice: Shut that horse up

Theo Wade: Too late

(Members of the tribe ride over to challenge Mercy and his men, both sides draw their weapons)

Mercy Justice: Which one is the leader?

Theo Wade: The one in front (sarcasm)

Mercy Justice: He dies first

Theo Wade: Wait

(The tribe stops and stares at Mercy and his men, The men make a path allowing them to walk through)

Theo Wade: Let's go before they change their mind.

(Mercy and his men walk through and head to the small town hoping to find Abbie)

Theo Wade: Mercy you have changed brother.

Mercy Justice: Why do you keep showing people mercy who have not done us the same?

Eugene: Maybe they just showed us mercy

Mercy Justice: The whole world against us! When will you understand that? When we find Abbie, I will shoot any rebel who gets in the way. Don't try to stop me Theo.

Theo Wade: I'm your brother until the end I just want you to protect your soul

Mercy Justice: Yea, and Jesus loves me, I know (sarcasm)

(The group arrives at Deacon Senior's church, a white man is across the street watching it, he rides off when he see's Deacon Senior)

Deacon Senior: Mr. Justice, welcome back to South Carolina

Mercy Justice: You have people watching your church

Deacon Senior: They are doing it to scare us. I sent all the women away. Abbie is not here. Just me and Moses.

Mercy Justice: We should leave and go join the women.

Deacon Senior: I built this church with my own hands! I am not running.

Mercy Justice: I've seen a lot of war and this is not a good place to fight. Can we go to the law man?

Deacon Senior: They are part of the White League. Judges, Sheriff's, Republicans and Democrats. Most of them don't even bother wearing the Klan robes.

(Down the road a shop owner is sweeping off his front porch and cleaning up the front of his shop.Gus and a few other men approach the store owner)

Gus: Good day sir.

Shop Owner: How can I help you Mr. Gus?

Gus: You have built this shop up real nice. Me and my men are thirsty, we want some drinks.

Shop Owner: Mr. Gus, I'm sorry to ask but you already owe me 2 dollars sir.

Gus: What did you just say boy?

Shop Owner: I didn't mean nothing by it sir, I just need the money.

Gus: You just embarrassed me in front of my friends. That wasn't very nice boy

Shop Owner: I apologize, cold drinks for everybody sir.

I didn't mean no harm

Gus: Sheriff, cover the door.

(The Sheriff walks over to the door)

Gus: We have to beat you now boy

Shop Owner: no, sir, please

(Gus walks over and hits the shop owner in the face. The shop owner falls to the ground. The others join in and beat on the shop owner. He crawls out of the shop as the men loot and take whatever they want. The Sheriff walks behind the shop owner as he crawls away. The sheriff shoots the shop owner)

People run out of close by shops and watch as the shop owner dies. The Sheriff walks over to make sure he is dead. Deacon Senior and others walk over to the shop.

Deacon Senior: Hey, you killed him!

Sheriff: He tried to rob his own store and I had to stop him.

Abbie: You're a liar!

Sheriff: You better move along or I will put a rope around your pretty neck.

(The Sheriff takes a step towards Abbie. Mercy raises his gun and points it at the Sheriff. Gus and the other men jump in but they are outnumbered.)

Sheriff: I will forgive you this time. You dare point that gun at a law man.

Mercy Justice: You are just another criminal, I don't see no law man.

Gus: See you soon nigger

(The men stand down and walk away with the stolen stuff the shop)

Deacon Senior: What are you doing here? Why did you come back Abbie?

Abbie: I came back for you.

1878

Theo Wade: We need to head back North as soon as possible. They are making it harder to move around down here. How long do we have to carry paper saying Mr. Sullivan gives us permission to walk around?

Mercy Justice: I'm sorry boys. Perhaps I have been selfish. Once the weather is warmer we will leave this place so that you boys can enjoy life.

Theo Wade: Did you ask her to marry you yet?

Mercy Justice: No

Theo Wade: The most feared black man in 7 states is scared of a little girl

Mercy Justice: I'm gonna put my foot up your hind parts Theo

(The group of men laugh)

(John P. Sullivan approaches)

John P. Sullivan: You guys are having way too much fun. What I'm I paying you for?

Theo Wade: You barely pay us

John P. Sullivan: What boy? Don't you sassy me! All of you, hand me your travel papers. You will get them back when the work is done.

(The men hand over the papers, John P. Sullivan walks away)

Eugene: How we free if we have to get permission to go where we want?

Mercy Justice: I'm sorry boys. One more month and we are gone. (scene)

(Mercy finds Abbie down near the water that night)

Abbie: Mr. Justice, hey

Mercy Justice: I want to show you something beautiful.

Abbie: I'm looking sir

Mercy Justice: Do you see that group of stars

Abbie: Yea

Mercy Justice: They're called Castor and Pollux, two Gemini twins

Abbie: Where did you learn that?

Mercy Justice: There's one more that should be around called Sirius

Abbie: You're a smart man

Mercy Justice: Be my wife

Abbie: What?

Mercy Justice: You want to go to Fisk, I will be near you.

Abbie: You sound like Moses

Mercy Justice: Did he…

Abbie: No man has ever touched me, not even our former masa Sullivan.

Mercy Justice: John P. Sullivan

Abbie: Yes

Mercy Justice: Good, I think I come to hate that man

(silence)

Abbie: He had my momma

Mercy Justice: I'm sorry dear

Abbie: Momma and Isabella coming back, now that Mr. Gus stopped watching us.

Mercy Justice: Was Isabella a slave?

Abbie: No, she came from that Spanish country. Her mamma was a slave, her father took her and ran to Spain. Mr. Sullivan never forgave them.

(Deacon Senior approaches)

Mercy Justice: Deacon

Deacon Senior: Abbie, go clean-up for supper

(Abbie walks away)

Deacon Senior: I come to like you Mercy. My daughter ain't for you.

Mercy Justice: Why is that?

Deacon Senior: You a heathen and you mock Jesus

Mercy Justice: How about we tell the truth for once?

Deacon Senior: Go ahead!

Mercy Justice: You let that cracker beat Jesus into you and touch your wife. I will not allow it for Abbie.

Deacon Senior: Why you…

Mercy Justice: Careful Deacon, I have killed men for less.

Deacon Senior: You don't scare me boy. Let me tell you something. 4 Years ago the Freedman's bank stole all of the churches money and my money. I worked hard to get more money! I feed that girl. You have a family one day and see how easy it is. I hit the masa and then Mable ain't got no husband. They would lynch me.

Mercy Justice: I'm not scared to die. That is the difference between us.

Deacon Senior: You would try to be brave and leave Abbie a widow?

Mercy Justice: I love her. I'll kill 100 men for her if I need to

Deacon Senior: You can love her during war, what about during peace?

Mercy Justice: You think white folk will give us peace?

Deacon Senior: Such a sad life to live and never have hope. Mable is back. Say your peace and then leave my property at once.

(Justice walks off angry)

(Deacon Senior sits down for dinner with Mable, Isabella, and Abbie)

Deacon Senior: I won't have that heathen back Abbie. He made a mockery of Jesus.

Abbie: I won't stay away from him

Deacon Senior: Did you kiss that boy?

Abbie: No

Mable: Enough, next time we eat, you will invite that man to dinner

Deacon Senior: Mable, now I'm the man

Mable: You the man. Strutting around like you King Tut!

Deacon Senior: Woman

Mable: Time for Abbie to be a woman

(Abbie covers her face)

Mable: This feeling is normal Abbie. I can see it all over your face

(The following day Mercy reports to the plantation to work, already in a bad mood)

Theo Wade: What's the matter Mercy?

Mercy Justice: I think we better off leaving now.

Eugene: Amen

(John P. Sullivan approaches)

John P. Sullivan: What did I tell you niggers about talking?

Mercy Justice: That's about all of the niggers I'm going to take from you!

(John P. Sullivan runs off, the men laugh)

Eugene: Back to the North I reckon

Mercy Justice: Fine, today is our last day

Theo Wade: Masa, I mean Mr. Sullivan has our travel papers

Mercy Justice: The constitution say we free! I don't need no papers with permission from no white man

(The men leave the plantation without collecting the rest of their wages. They gather their horses and money that they saved from the war. Mercy decides to head off to say goodbye to Abbie when he is stopped by the Sheriff and John P. Sullivan)

John P. Sullivan: That's one of them!

Sheriff: Where are the rest of your people boy?

Mercy Justice: Sir, we are leaving your county for good.

John P. Sullivan: too late boy

Sheriff: Walking around without permission from a white

man is against the Black Code. South Carolina gives me permission to lynch you. I'm going to cut you some slack boy. Have you ever heard of convict leasing? (scene)

(The men wait for Mercy Justice to return but he doesn't. Moses approaches)

Moses: The Sheriff got your boy

Theo Wade: Oh no, what do we do?

Eugene: We head north

Theo Wade: We can't leave mercy

Eugene: We all become prisoners then, we have no papers

Theo Wade: We all become prisoners then! Moses can you store our horses and money?

Moses: Yes

(Thomas, Ben, Eugene, Virgil, Leonard, and Theo head into the town. They walk up to the Sheriff's office and start signing)

Group: (Sings gospel song)

(The Sheriff walks out)

Sheriff: Hey boys, I see we got more bodies for our convict leasing program…

(The convict leasing program was a new form of slavery. It was the loop hole in the 13th Amendment abolished slavery and involuntary Servitude except as punishment for a crime. In the south they just simply made everything black people (especially black men) did was considered a crime.)

Black Codes

(Deacon Senior reads the new Black Codes to his church)

No Negro may carry a weapon except members of the military (A violation of the second amendment)

Negros may not assemble without the presents of a white person (A violation of the fourteenth Amendment)

All Negroes are required to be in service of some white person (A violation of the fourteenth Amendment)

No Negro is allowed to preach to a congregation without permission (A violation of the first amendment)

No Negro is permitted to rent or own a house in certain parishes (A violation of the fourteenth Amendment)

A one drop rule is now in effect adding all Mulatto to the black code

No white is permitted to marry a Negro

You now need a license from a judge to be a shop keeper and for Negroes it cost 100.00 (A violation of the fourteenth amendment and Civil Rights Act of 1866.)

All public transportation is to be segregated

(The congregation gasp)

Mable: If these codes violate our rights granted by the constitution how can they do this?

Deacon Senior: I don't know. I have to write my friend in Washington and let them know.

Thomas, Ben, Eugene, Virgil, Leonard, and Theo join

Mercy Justice on a chain gang convict leasing program clearing trees.

Eugene: Mercy

Mercy Justice: You got caught too

Eugene: We wanted to get caught.

(A guard approaches)

Guard: You boys shut your mouths and get to work.

Mercy Justice: This was your plan?

(Theo falls to the ground and starts yelling)

Theo Wade: My leg boss sir! My leg

Guard 2: You dumb nigger

(Leonard, who was the biggest of them all, wrapped his chain around the guard's neck and then knocked him out with his bare hands. Guard 1 attempts to run over, Mercy trips him and then grabs his shotgun knocking him out)

Mercy Justice: Eugene, get the keys. Thank you. We have to head north. (scene)

(The Sheriff learns about the two guards and pays Deacon Senior a visit)

Deacon Senior: Sheriff, how can I help you sir?

Sheriff: I was told Mercy Justice hung out here around your church.

Deacon Senior: We haven't seen him in a long time

Sheriff: He escaped a chain gang, injured two guards

Deacon Senior: Was he arrested for breaking one of your unconstitutional black codes?

Sheriff: Shut your mouth, now. Enough, I think it's time to show you all who is boss down here.

(Badger sits on his front porch awaiting the arrival of the Sheriff.)

Badger: You seem angry Sheriff

Sheriff: Damn jungle bunnies are making a fool of us! Are you going to just sit there? The great Badger Long. (sarcasm)

Badger: I am patiently waiting for word from Washington.

Sheriff: Well I won't keep bowing to them! They can't keep doing what they want. We have laws. We are a nation of laws.

(Paul heads to the home of Deacon Senior)

Paul: I'm afraid that time is approaching again Senior.

Deacon Senior: What do you mean Paul?

Paul: The Posse Comitatus Act was just signed by President Rutherford B. Hayes.

Deacon Senior: What is it?

Paul: It prevents the army from coming down here to protect you guys from The White League. Listen, I feel like I owe you the truth. A commission of white men, Republicans and Democrats met to decide the election. Rutherford B. Hayes won and neither party will ever really help the Negro. You have rights on paper but you don't have rights.

Deacon Senior: You was just some innocent witness Paul?

Paul: I am so sorry for what we did to you and your people. Forgive me Deacon. Nobody is coming to save you. Nobody can hear your screams.

Deacon Senior: There is no forgiveness. You and your kind will feel the wrath of the Lord.

Paul: Sorry

(Paul walks off)

(June 18th 1878 President Rutherford B. Hayes signs the Posse Comitatus Act)
The White League

Gus: Gentleman, welcome to our local chapter of The White Man's League. First order of business.

Rufus: A group of niggers attacked two law men in the convict leasing program. We can't allow this to stand.

Badger: The day has come. Time to line them up and hang em high

(The White League head over to the poor side of town where many black farmers and cooks worked. They grab Moses out of his quarters. The people step outside to see what all of the commotion was about)

Badger: Is this the one?

Olga: That's him, he raped me! The nigger raped me!

Moses: No, I didn't rape her! I swear to God.

Olga: You fucking nigger, die! (Olga spits on Moses)

(Abbie runs home to get her father)

Abbie: Daddy, they're going to lynch Moses. They said he raped Olga.

Deacon Senior: Oh, no

Mable: Did you know he was laying with that white girl?

Deacon Senior: I told him to stop

Mable: Damn you Senior

(Deacon Senior, Abbie, and Mable run to the town square to try to stop the lynching)

Badger: Do you have any other words before you die?

Moses: Sir I…

(Badger slaps the horse and it takes off, Moses's neck snaps and he hangs as the crowd watches him die. Deacon Senior tries to run up to cut Moses down but Badger pushes him to the ground)

Badger: I want you niggers to know, that for now on the white man is your God! You will eat when we say eat. You will sleep when we say sleep, you will work when we say work and you will die when we say die. The government won't save you this time!

Deacon Senior goes back home in a rage. He throws things around in his church out of anger and frustration at the death of Moses.

Deacon Senior: Why God?

Abbie: Daddy it's going to be alright

Deacon Senior: None of this is right. Why are they so evil Lord? Why don't you destroy them? I know your power!

Mable: I got you baby. I got you.

(The two women hug on Deacon Senior as he sits on the floor in tears.)

(In the Mississippi valley a yellow fever epidemic sweeps the state killing men, women, and children. The death toll is like no other since the black plague in Europe)

Down the way Paul rushes to find Badger.

Paul: Have you seen Badger? I need Badger now!

Badger: Kid, what do you want?

Paul: The Yellow Fever hit, people are dying all over Mississippi.

Badger: Yellow fever?

Paul: You're whole family died. Your mother and sisters have passed away

(Badger sits and drinks some whiskey)

Badger: Those niggers and their voodoo magic. Evil witch black people magic

Paul: It was a random epidemic. It killed thousands

Badger: Don't you see how evil these black cowards are? Using their magic to kill thousands of good Christian whites. I am going to kill them all.

Paul: Badger, this is going too far. I think you should sit for a minute

Badger: Leave me. Go!

(The newly freed people got some time to mourn Moses and attempt to live a normal life while Badger and the White League decided to take a break. Badger was filled with rage but stayed in doors for the remainder of the year drinking himself to sleep.)

1879

Black Exodus

(Black Americans begin to flee the South by the thousands due to Jim Crow and Black Codes. Many of them end up in Kansas after finding out that Liberia would be too hard due to logistics)

Mercy Justice: I finally made it

Theo Wade: What took you so long?

Mercy Justice: I was stranded in St. Louis. They weren't too happy to see Negroes either.

Theo Wade: We managed to buy little scraps of land, most of the good land already was given to the whites here.

Mercy Justice: I guess something is better than nothing at all.

Eugene: Well, we have a job for you if you want it

Mercy Justice: Thank you old friend

(Mercy Justice settles in and attempts to forget about Abbie and the others. He doesn't make much but has savings from when he was in the army. Most of the group find themselves staying in Kansas)

(Mercy is chopping wood and having a conversation with his two most trusted friends)

Mercy Justice: Have you ever wondered what life could have been.

Theo Wade: Maybe someday you visit Fisk and she will

be there.

Eugene: Maybe you find a good woman in Kansas.

Theo Wade: He want Abbie, ever since he smelled that girl hair he has been running around sad.

Mercy Justice: Maybe someday she goes to Fisk and I will see her there. South Carolina is no good for us.

Eugene: You hurt too many white folks

Mercy Justice: I didn't hurt enough

Theo Wade: Have you ever heard of John Brown? He was white and he killed a whole lot of white folks, not because of their color but because they wanted to keep slaves. It is evil to treat humans worse than dirt. Jesus said love thy neighbor.

Mercy Justice: Is that why they want to live far away from us?

(laughing)

Mercy Justice: It's good to be among you guys.

Eugene: Stop mopping around, let's see what Kansas has to offer.

(The men head out for a night on the town. They stop at a local saloon for drinks)

Theo Wade: I'm buying both of you guys a drink.

Eugene: See, I told you there would be women in Kansas

(The guys approach a group of women)

Eugene: Hey, my name is Eugene and this is Theo. How are you women?

Sue: I am doing fine, why is your friend so quiet over there?

Eugene: Because he needs a lady. You should go say hi

Sue: My momma said I should not be in a grown man face.

Eugene: Well, you're grown and on your own now little lady

(Sue sits next to Mercy Justice)

Sue: So much pain in those eyes sir

Mercy Justice: I'm happy, just don't look it, that's all. It seems so crowded here. A lot of us coming at once.

Sue: We are moving to Nicodemus. They say it's a place for our people. Did you meet Pap?

Mercy Justice: Pap?

Sue: Mr. Singleton, we just call him Pap. He the one told us about Kansas. When we get to Nicodemus everything will be fine.

Mercy Justice: No

Sue: Only three of you?

Mercy Justice: There was more.

Sue: What happened to the others?

Mercy Justice: Yellow fever

Leonard: Mercy? Mercy Justice?

Mercy Justice: Big Leonard, what are you doing alive? I thought you died?

Leonard: I was too sick to cross over, but I didn't have yellow fever.

Mercy Justice: A miracle

Leonard: nope, nope, Virgil, Ben, and Thomas all dead. They "dead dead"! Not coming back dead.

Mercy Justice: Leonard, I get it. Well, I'm glad you're alive.

Leonard: Are you going to Nicodemus with us?

Mercy Justice: us?

Leonard: Sue here is friends with my Missy.

Mercy Justice: You found a woman?

Leonard: Brother, I found the woman. The world's best woman.

Mercy Justice: I'm happy for you. We go to Nicodemus!

South Carolina

Badger: The white League has maintained law in this land. We was just lawless a few short years ago.

Paul: I have to go guys.

(Paul leaves)

Gus: Paul doesn't have the stomach for keeping the niggers in order.

Badger: I hung a few 10, 20 I lost count. Welcome to Badger world.

Gus: Your methods work…

Badger: What?

Gus: The nigger that killed my Papi! He attacked the law. Why is he still alive? He caused trouble and then fled

Rufus: His name is Mercy Justice. We don't know where he lives.

Badger: Well, bring him out of hiding

Rufus: How?

Badger: Jesus, I have to do everything around here. They say he always around the preacher's little girl. Hang that nigger. (scene)

(Isabella practices singing gospel when a group of men approach the church)

Gus: We didn't come for you. We want Abbie

Deacon Senior: What you want with my little girl?

Badger: We want to have a word with her

Deacon Senior: She left South Carolina

Badger: What a shame. Maybe we hang the half Spaniard girl

Deacon Senior: Maybe you leave my church.

Isabella: Deacon. No

Deacon Senior: You people have so much bad things to

say about Negro's but you are the most violent people walking this Earth. Every week you hang someone just because you can. This evil country gives you permission to "runamuck"

Badger: Oh Deacon, you bring me joy

(Paul runs into the church)

Paul: Please Badger, don't do it. Everyone loves Deacon Senior. He's a peaceful man.

Badger: You traitor

Paul: I know you came for Abbie, she ain't here! She went to school. Please Badger. Please.

Badger: You are a lucky man Deacon. We shall return sir

(The men leave except Paul)

Paul: There is nothing I can do to atone for this Deacon. I helped create this evil.

Isabella: Deacon!

(Badger and his men start shooting the church up. Isabella is shot in the head and instantly dies. Badger and his men reload and keep firing.)

Paul: Here is my gun Deacon. I didn't bring any extra bullets. Get out of South Carolina.

Deacon Senior: Thank you Paul.

Paul: You think I'll go to heaven now?

Deacon Senior: No.

(silence)

Paul: Tell Abbie I tried to be a good person.

(Paul gets up and walks to the door as the bullets come flying in. Deacon senior opens one of the pews and gets in with the gun. Paul drops to the ground with bullet holes in his body)

Gus: No way they survived that. Rufus, go check

(Rufus steps over Paul's dead body. He spots Isabella but not the Deacon.)

Rufus: The preacher must have ran off.

Gus: Damn

Badger: Find the Deacon and hang him

Rufus: He is a man of God

Badger: This is South Carolina. God won't save him.

(Deacon Senior waits for them to leave and then hops out of the pew)

Nicodemus, Kansas
1880

Mercy Justice: Sue can you fetch me some water?

Sue: There was nothing here when the first freedmen arrived in 1877 from Kentucky. Now we have churches and schools and businesses. If we just keep building, when the railroad comes this can be a place for Negro people from all over.

Mercy Justice: I like the idea. They are building a hotel down the road. So many skilled free men and women. You have Negro women who couldn't even read now they are school teachers.

Eugene: Hey Mercy, I see you found a way to start making some money.

Mercy Justice: Eugene, thank you friend

Eugene: We are our own family now. You like my brother Mercy. Leonard and Theo too.

Mercy Justice: Brothers, not so good brothers, but hell I'll take it

(The men laugh)

(Mercy Justice and Sue decide to jump the broom, an old tradition used when the slaves would get married. Leonard also was married to Missy and the two had a child on the way. They finally found themselves settling down and becoming family.)

Nicodemus grew in population. They had about 600

residents, many skilled and educated black people. They had stores, hotels, schools, churches, and areas to hang out. The working poor built homes that went into the ground called "dug outs". Many people owned land and homes. Nicodemus was not perfect but they lived free of black codes and Jim Crow.

(The people gathered to dance and celebrate the opening of a hotel, Mercy danced and danced with Sue. He had finally found some degree of happiness.)

Mercy Justice: A lot of nearby whites are complaining that too many Negro's are coming here.

Sue: We have the second Amendment here. They wouldn't be dumb enough to attack us. You are safe Mercy.

Mercy Justice: I did some things in the past.

Sue: My Daddy told me some men have to get a little rough. We can't survive without you.

Mercy Justice: You make me happy.

Sue: You learned how to love somebody

Mercy Justice: Abbie?

Sue: No!

Mercy Justice: Behind you, Abbie

(Abbie tracked Mercy Justice down)

Abbie: Hey Mercy

(The tension is clearly building between Sue and Abbie.

Abbie steps outside to talk to Mercy)

Mercy Justice: I thought you went to Fisk?

Abbie: I went to Howard instead. I live in Washington

Mercy Justice: Why travel to Kansas?

Abbie: My Daddy is in danger.

Mercy Justice: He needs to leave South Carolina. Nothing there but evil.

Abbie: He can't get out. They will shoot him on site. Can you help me?

Mercy Justice: I have a family now…

Abbie: Finally got you a pretty wife.

Mercy Justice: Sorry

(Sue checks on the two)

Sue: Is everything ok? Do you need some punch? (with attitude)

Mercy Justice: No punch!

Abbie: How is Theo and the rest of them?

Mercy Justice: Ben, Thomas and Virgil died. The Yellow fever got them.

Abbie: I'm so sorry

(Abbie hugs Mercy until Sue gives a hard stare)

Abbie: Senior won't make it out alive. My Momma puts her life in danger to sneak him food and water. I'm going to get my Daddy. Enjoy your wife. She is beautiful.

(Abbie starts to walk away)

Mercy Justice: Wait…Eugene…

Eugene: I'm with you Mercy, until the end.

Theo Wade: I'm with you until the end

Mercy Justice: Leonard, you got a "youngin" on the way

Leonard: I'm coming, we brothers until the end

Sue: I will go in Leonard's place. Leonard, stay and raise your baby

Leonard: can you shoot?

Sue: I'm from Kentucky, all we do is shoot

Abbie: It's settled

Eugene: Get low, Get low brother

Mercy Justice: Get low, get low brother

Theo Wade: Get low, get low brother

Sue: The Free Will Rise Again!

(The group packs up and gets ready to head back to South Carolina, leaving behind the newly found Nicodemus.)

The End of Act 2

ACT 3

MJ Senior checks on his fathers damaged church to make sure it is ok. He pays close attention to Rufus who is watching the Church. MJ. Runs back home and quickly closes the door.

MJ. Senior: Daddy, they are still watching the church.

Deacon Senior: Thank you son, go with your mother to get food today. I'll be fine here alone.

MJ. Senior: You never go outside Daddy. You need sun and to be able to walk around

Deacon Senior: If anyone ask you make sure that you tell them I am missing.

(The Sheriff rides up to check on Rufus)

Rufus: He is either in the church or in the home. I can feel that beady eyed nigger watching us.

Sheriff Dudley: He will show his face eventually. Do not touch his property.

Rufus: Got it

(Sue watches Deacon Senior's house until Rufus leaves.

She see's Mable and MJ walk out of the home. She approaches the two.)

Sue: Hey

Mable: Can I help you young lady?

Sue: Here is a gift from your daughter

(Sue gives a suit case to Mable. Mable takes it into the house and opens it. The suitcase is filled with guns and bullets. Mable sighs)

Sue meets the rest of the group at a close by lodging area.

Mercy Justice: Did you deliver the package?

Sue: Yes.

Mercy Justice: We will get your father when night falls.

Abbie: Sue and I should go get him. We are not "wanted"

Eugene: No way

Abbie: I am a grown woman. I can do this

Mercy Justice: You and Sue travel the main way. We will travel through the woods. Be careful.

(MJ and Mable pick up some food from the local shop. They are trying to make it home before it gets too dark. Rufus approaches the two.)

Rufus: Where is Deacon Senior Mable? He's wanted for killing Paul

Mable: My husband would never kill Paul. We all know who shot Paul and Isabella

Rufus: What did you say nigger?

MJ Senior: Leave my Moma alone!

Rufus: You shut your mouth boy

Mable: Please Mr. Rufus, we suffered enough

Rufus: Maybe I keep you company while your husband is missing. Maybe we give you to Mr. Sullivan.

Mable: You shut your mouth

Rufus: Sheriff, take her to jail for threatening a white man

MJ. Senior: Stay away from my momma!

(MJ pulls a gun, Sheriff Dudley and two of his men pull their guns as well)

Sheriff: Now we get to hang you boy

(One of the deputies hits MJ with a rifle. The men grab him and carry him to the town square to lynch him. Mable starts begging for mercy as they set MJ up to be hung.)

Rufus: You're in real trouble now

Mable: Please sir, have mercy sir

(A small angry crowd watched the Sheriff as they put MJ on a horse to lynch him)

Rufus: We are going to hang your son and give you back to Mr. Sullivan where you belong!

(A shot lands and goes right through Rufus's skull, Rufus drops. The horse is startled and takes off. Mable grabs her son's legs and holds him up. Mercy heads over with a knife to cut the boy down. Sheriff Dudley reaches for his gun. He gets shot in the neck and drops to the ground. The two deputies place their hands in the air to surrender. Sue appears from out of nowhere holding her rifle. Mercy cuts the boy down.)

Mercy Justice: You tried to kill a child.

Deputy 1: It wasn't us

Mercy lays an object on the ground and unwraps it. He pulls out an Axe. Eugene tries to stop him.

Eugene: Mercy!

Mercy Justice: No mercy, only justice

Mercy swings his axe and chops the first deputy in the throat. He falls to the ground with half of his neck hacked off and bleeds out on the ground. The second deputy tries to run but Justice pulls out his gun and shoots him in the back.

Mercy Justice: Go get Deacon Senior.

Abbie: Where are you going?

Mercy Justice: I have to get to Badger before he gets to you.

Sue: Let me come with you.

Mercy Justice: I love you. I have to go alone.

Sue: No sad "goodbye" just make it back to me husband

Mercy picks up his bloody axe and covers his face. He walks off in his own direction. Sue wipes her eyes and then re loads her rifle.

Abbie: Let's hurry up and get out of here.

Eugene, Theo, Abbie, Sue, Mable, and MJ make it to the house. Sue goes in to check on the suit case while MJ goes to get his father. He finds Deacon Senior on the ground dead. The suitcase is empty. The poor deacon died with is eyes open.

MJ Senior: Father!

Gus and The White League stand outside of Deacon Seniors home and fire bullets into the house. Everybody ducks for cover. The men reload and keep firing.

Eugene: We have to get the women and children out of here. They'll just keep shooting.

Theo Wade: There's no telling how many of them outside. They're shooting from different directions.

Sue: We're stronger together

Abbie: They killed my Father!

(Abbie breaks down crying)

Sue: We still have to get your mother and brother out. Don't give up on me now!

Eugene: How do we get out?

Abbie: MJ go into the pantry and don't come out until we get you! Crawl.

Abbie grabs a mirror and tries to see if she can see anyone approaching the house.

Abbie: It's getting too dark.

Gus: We can stand out here and shoot all night long! Whooo!

Abbie: Sounds like Gus.

Sue: We take the front and Eugene and Theo will take the back. If we don't fight back we're all going to die.

Gus: Why didn't you just go back to Africa?

Sue: That's right keep talking (whispers to herself)

Gus: Welcome to the race war. I told them damn Yankees we would solve the Nigger problem. Just like little bugs! H…

(Sue sends a shot in the direction of Gus. She hits him in the chest and knocks him off his horse.)

White League member 1: They shot Gus!

White League member 2: Kill them all! Burn the house down and smoke them out.

The men break the windows and toss objects into the home setting it on fire.

Abbie grabs her brother and mother and they gather together.

Sue: Abbie, you and your family go last… see you soon

(Abbie nods)

Sue breaks a side window instead of going out the front or the back. She covers the right while Eugene and Theo cover the left of them. One by one they "drop" members of the white league as they run to the side of the house to back each other up. As they shift to the side, Abbie, Mable, and MJ go out the front door during the distraction. Sue unloads a revolver, since she does not have time to reload she grabs a revolver off one of the dead men and keeps shooting. Abbie has a clear shot towards the woods and tries to take it but someone screams "there they are". Two of the members of the white league break off and head towards Abbie. Abbie aims her revolver and hits one but the other shooter gets a clear shot until Mable gets in the way taking the shot for her daughter.

Abbie: Mama!

Abbie empties the revolver on the man who shot her mother. MJ and Abbie drag Mable into the cover of the nearby woods area. Eugene helps Theo clear the other side but one of the remaining members of the white league rushes and tackles Eugene into the burning house. Theo shoots the attacker in the back. The remaining members run away after being met with the resistance. Eugene is badly burned and can't be moved by Theo.

Theo Wade: Eugene say something man! Don't die on me man. Somebody help! Somebody help!

(One of the onlookers runs and gets help. They attempt to treat Eugene who is badly burnt.)

Witness: This man needs a Doctor. Somebody else rides into town to seek medical attention for Eugene.

Abbie: Theo, you can stay with Eugene. I have to get my family out of here.

Theo Wade: Go Abbie. Thank you.

Abbie goes back to help Mable up but she has passed away from the gunshot. Abbie goes into shock and can't move until her brother MJ gives her a hard nudge. The two scream for help until others show up and then they disappear.

MJ Senior: Father's body is burnt. How are we going to bury them? We can't just leave them like that.

Abbie: I promise they will get a burial. Right now I have to get you out of here. (scene)

(Olga fetches some water and then heads back to her house. She fixes some food and then sits down to eat. Mercy Justice sneaks up behind her with his axe. She turns around and screams.)

Mercy Justice: I know, scream again and I'll take your head off. Who told you to lie on Moses?

Olga: I didn't lie, He raped me.

Mercy Justice: Who told you to set up Moses... Who?!

Olga: It was John Sullivan.

Mercy Justice: Why?

Olga: Because I loved him.

Mercy Justice: Put your hands on the table where I can see them! Now!

(Olga places her hands on the table.)

Olga: I don't have any weapons. I'm sorry!

Mercy Justice: Who is John Sullivan to you?

Olga: Nobody.

(Mercy slams his axe chopping off the right hand of Olga, she screams. Mercy picks up her hand and places it in a bag and then leaves. Olga falls on the ground screaming. Her right hand struck off. (Scene)

(John Sullivan sits on his front porch eating peaches. It was his way of relaxing in the evening. Abbie approaches from the east and Sue approaches from the west. They both point their guns at Mr. Sullivan.)

John P. Sullivan: Wait!

Abbie: You put your hands on my Mother! How do you live with yourself?

John P. Sullivan: You shouldn't have been created. You mistake of God! Everything about you is wrong.

Abbie: Who are you to decide? There is no God in you!

Sue: Any last words?

John P. Sullivan: White…..over…..black….. and when you kill me, you will still be a nigger.

(The two women shoot John P. Sullivan repeatedly until he falls dead.)

Sue: Are you going back to Washington?

Abbie: Eventually.

Sue: We best be going

(The two women get MJ and they all take Mr. Sullivan's

horses and ride off. John P. Sullivan lays dead with his eyes open). (scene)

(Mercy Justice decides to pay Badger a visit. He waits outside of The White Leagues meeting place until it begins to clear out. Badger shakes a few people's hands and then goes back inside.)

Badger: Did you hear? They killed the Sheriff and Rufus.

Jerry: We need more men

Badger: A bunch of unruly animals

Jerry: I'll be here with you until you decide to go

Badger: I'm going to hurt them. Sweet Jesus I'm going to hurt them. America will give me an award for killing so many niggers. I am going to enjoy it. You can go home Jerry.

Jerry: What if they come to get you?

Badger: Jerry, how long have you known me? They're already here.

(Jerry walks outside and has a look around. He gets on his horse and rides away. Badger walks outside and spits out his snuff. He looks around and then goes back inside. Justice comes out of hiding across the road and heads to the building. He whips out his handy axe and opens the door, creeping inside. He follows the whistling of Badger)

Badger: Come on in boy. I know you're here.

Mercy Justice: You knew I was coming but you chose to face me alone?

Badger: Who said I was alone?

(Leonard walks out from around the corner and points a gun at Mercy)

Mercy Justice: Leonard! What?

Leonard: We already lost, and you keep trying to fight a lost cause.

Mercy Justice: Why brother…Why?

Leonard: Money. They can't have Negroes like ya'll fighting back. I left a day after you left.

Mercy Justice: Traitor…

Leonard: You ain't no better than me. You left me sick in St. Louis. You would have let me die!

(Mercy rushes Leonard but Leonard gets a shot off first striking him in the midsection. The two men start rolling and fighting on the ground. Badger watches with delight. Mercy screams in pain as Leonard hits him in the midsection. He points his gun at Mercy's head for a kill shot but Mercy grabs the gun. The two men struggle over the gun. Mercy finally get the upper hand for a second pulling the trigger and blowing a hole through Leonard's head. Mercy drops the gun and Badger kicks it away)

Badger: Yee haw, are we having fun now boy?!

(Badger shoots Mercy again.)

Mercy: (Muffled response)

Badger: You just couldn't accept your place in this world. You animals are not smart enough! If God wanted you to win you would have won. You lose boy. I was always in control. I am going to kill you and then I am going to kill your nigger wife. Leonard told me where she lives.

Mercy Justice: No!

Badger: You shut your mouth!

(Badger grabs Mercy by the face)

Badger: Shut your monkey mouth!

Mercy Justice: (Muffled response)

Badger: Go ahead, say your last words.

(Badger leans in to hear Mercy. Mercy stabs him through the throat with a blade he pulled from his boot. Badger falls backwards shooting in the air. Mercy starts crawling towards the door. He gathers his strength and keeps moving toward the door. Mercy reaches the door in time to see the beautiful sky before he dies. He looks for the constellations in the sky as he slowly drifts off, truly free)

Mercy's final letter

Abbie, I love you more than you will ever know. I could never accept your God or your father. I was prepared to pretend so that you would love me. I think you loved me anyway. I never stopped loving you or even your crazy father, who tried to drown me. I won't be coming back from South Carolina. I have already been given a vision. My final resting place will be South Carolina. I had a dream that I died looking up at the sky. I felt something like God, but I couldn't understand it. It was telling me everything would be fine. The human soul burns even longer than the stars. To tell the truth, I was afraid the whole time. I just kept going. It was like my destination was already set for me, like I was born dead. I know you will make it out and my letter will find you. Please don't tell Sue. I never meant to love you instead of her. I guess that makes me a human. Please live your life. Fall in love with a man and have children. You will be an educated mother. You will be strong and brave and everything I saw when we met.

The Free Will Rise Again!

Mercy…

Over 4,000 free black people were lynched and thousands more shot or beat to death due to actions of government at all levels.

2020

A nicely dressed young man stands before congress during a study about reparations set to go nowhere.

Congressman Mitch: Todays white people didn't own slaves. I think black people should just get over it now.

E.J. Wade: It is because of ignorant comments such as the one you just made that I got involved in this mission. Way too many people have the fact pattern wrong when it comes to Jim Crow.

Congressman Mitch: Are you saying that I don't know history sir?

E.J. Wade: To make a claim that Black Americans who are Descendants of Slavery and Jim Crow should simply forget about it and walk away suggest you don't fully grasp the history.

Congressman Mitch: It is history not present.

E.J. Wade: The commission of 1876 is still in full effect today. African people were emancipated in 1863 right?

Congressman Mitch: Yes

E.J. Wade: Traitors of this nation murdered a sitting president, but before he died he signed the 13th Amendment correct?

Congressman Mitch: Yes

E.J. Wade: Then came the Civil Rights Act of 1866.

Congressman Mitch: Then the 14th Amendment. I know the history sir.

E.J. Wade: Allow us to look over the language of the 14th Amendment.

(All persons born or naturalized in the United States and subject to its jurisdiction thereof, are Citizens of the United States and of the state wherein they reside.)

EJ Wade: Stop. "Citizens of the United States AND! Of the state wherein they reside.

E.J. Wade: Does the 14th Amendment declare free black people to be citizens of the state in which they reside?

Congressman Mitch: Correct

No state shall make or enforce any law which shall abridge the privileges or immunities of citizens of the United States.

EJ Wade: Stop! Repeat No state shall make or enforce any law which shall abridge the privileges or immunities of citizens of the United States. Did states make black codes and Jim Crow Laws that only targeted black citizens?

Congressman Mitch: Yes

Nor shall any state deprive a person of pursuit of life, liberty, or property, without due process of law.

E.J. Wade: I don't understand how you can make a "States Rights" argument at this point when the 14th Amendment is telling you what a state can't do, yet they did it.

Nor deny to any person under it's jurisdiction the equal protection of the laws.

E.J. Wade: Shall we continue to the 15th Amendment?

Congressman Mitch: No, please, no more Amendments. I know the constitution sir.

E.J. Wade: Very well let's move on to United States V. Cruikshank which arose from the Colfax Massacre of 1873. The rights to assemble and bear arms, the first and second Amendments were violated. The Supreme Court ruled that this only applies to Federal law, not states or private citizens. We just read the 14th amendment which clearly charged the states with the same responsibilities as the federal government right? What about citizens, can an angry black mob go into a white church, snatch the Bible from a white preachers hand and beat him with it to stop him from engaging in freedom of his religion or right to assemble?

Congressman Mitch: No but local laws should protect the preacher.

E.J. Wade: What if they refuse? In Cruikshank 100 people were killed and nobody was charged with murder? They shot people who surrendered and put their weapons down.

E.J. Wade: Justice Clifford gave a dissenting opinion that section 5 of the 14th Amendment gives congress the power to enforce the 14th Amendment. Now people are stating the Court got it wrong because the rights of white gun owners are being challenged today because of it.

Congressman Mitch: Noted many people disagree with Cruikshank and parts of it have been overturned. Ladies and gentleman we need to take a 30 minute recess, I will see you all back here at 12:30.

Congress is back in session

Congresswoman Walters: The timeline you gave highlighted that sometimes the states and the United States got it wrong when it came to protecting the rights of citizens. This is why you are arguing for reparations?

E.J. Wade: Here is where the timeline gets tricky. A group of 15 white men meet in 1876 to form a commission to decide an election. They strike a deal or a compromise awarding 20 electoral votes to Rutherford B. Hayes making him president over Tilden. Not one black representative was present. A deal was struck to not only pull back federal troops but to "allow the southern states to deal with Negro people as they please".

At the creation of the 14th Amendment all citizens are equal citizens but this commission and all levels of government continued to use race and drew distinct racial lines or they played the "race card" to circumvent all of the rights granted under the 14th and 15th Amendment to the constitution. They allowed the states to create Jim Crow laws and black codes that specifically targeted black peopled for approximately 88 years. We should have never needed a Civil Rights Act of 1964. We had to spend time, lives, and resources fighting to get something enforced that was put in place almost a century prior to but white personnel who work for the government just refused to enforce it. The government, at all levels picked winners and losers. Black people were forced into being 2nd class citizens at gunpoint. Over 4,000 people lynched and thousands more shot to death. As a matter of fact we weren't even 2nd class citizens. Someone who needs a piece of paper from a white citizen giving them permission to live is slavery. You enslaved citizens, you went around a two-thirds majority and wiped your butts with the constitution.

(Congressman: Watch your language sir)

Today you use the 14th Amendment for Immigrants far and wide, and hand them a copy of the constitution, using the 14th Amendment to grant them and their children born on U.S. soil rights that you denied black people who the 14th amendment was created for in the first place. Also whenever resources are appropriated under the guise of fixing past wrongs you use broad vague terms like "people of color" and "minority" making sure that Descendants of Jim Crow get very little of the resources. You also granted white Immigrants like Italians and Asian Immigrants full rights that you denied us even though we built the country they migrated to and the spirit of the law of the 14th Amendment was for us! Let me know if I missed something.

Native Americans have been allowed to violate provisions in treaties that state Freedmen were supposed to get some of the resources from those treaties. The largest beneficiary of

Affirmative Action in hiring has become white women, who are the majority of the American population, not numerical minorities. We have fought in every war since the Civil war yet people from countries that have bombed the United States get more protected rights over us today. Well "people of color" did not get enslaved or lynched, neither did "minorities" but black people.

Here is what we are demanding and here is what is owed to us, through our unique justice claim. Keep in mind this is besides the justice claim for slavery itself. This particular claim is due to the 88 years of the government at all levels simply choosing to ignore our rights and granting rights to everyone else but us. This claim is for placing free citizens back into "neo slavery". This claim is pertaining to the revoking of citizenship, in an unofficial and devious way which was illegal and unconstitutional at the tune of billions being lost from a black economy

Supreme Court Justices should no longer hold a seat for longer than 8 years. A president can win 2 terms and serve 8 years. There is no reason Supreme Court justices should hold more power than a president. The 5 Supreme Court Justices Nathan Clifford, Joseph Bradley, Samuel Freeman Miller, Steven Johnson Field, and William Strong were present at the commission and that tainted any decision made by the Supreme Court that denied protection under the 14th Amendment. The Supreme Court has become a political weapon to take rights instead of engaging in interpretation of the law. The blood of Black America is on their hands.

Black Americans are stake holders in this nation. We are

the foundation and builders of this nation who fought to keep it together when others rebelled. We have less than 1% of the nation's wealth. Descendants of slave owners and rebels along with some newly arrived immigrants have changed the narrative to " lazy blacks" from the actual reality of a president being murdered and free citizens being re enslaved. The legal damages for the period referred to as Jim Crow and Black Codes should be no less than 100 billion dollars PER YEAR! from 1877 until 1964. This should account for land that black Americans had to abandon to run from the Klan and the White League. This includes the mistreatment of black veterans who fought in every war. The economic loss and lives lost from mob violence allowed by the states and courts are also included.

In order to prevent further back door deals and "handshakes" both political parties and the Supreme Court need to issue an apology to Black Americans. Black Americans who are descendants of Jim Crow are to be removed from vague and broad legal language such as "minority" and "people of color" and placed in our own category alone as Descendants of Slavery and Jim Crow. Any other group should have to make their own justice claim. No person with ties to a white supremacist group or that is associated with any white supremacist group such as the Klan or the White League shall be allowed to be law enforcement over Black Americans who are Descendants of Jim Crow and Black Codes. New Immigrants should have to learn about the 14th Amendment, the history of the 14th Amendment and the violations of the 14th Amendment that they enjoy today. The history must include Black Americans relationship to the 14th

Amendment.

Congresswoman Walters: What if we simply decide to ignore these demands?

E.J. Wade: As a descendant of Jim Crow and Black Codes I and about 43 million more of us will vote you out and put in a government that will. We will form a Constitutional Party and run our own candidates to disrupt the crooked politics of Washington.

Congresswoman Walters: You're group is a minority, 14 percent of the population at best.

E.J. Wade: The Japanese, The European Jews, The families of 9/11 victims and Native Americans are a smaller minority and you fight tooth and nail and have fought historically to resolve their justice claims and keep in mind the families of 9/11 were attacked by terrorist and the Japanese Internment lasted from 1942 until 1946. That is 4 years versus our 88. The United States paid 20,000 in reparations each..We have received 0 dollars and 0 cents. This not because our claim is not legitimate, it is because you are keeping with the compromise of 1876.

Congresswoman Walters: Many of the people who lived under Jim Crow are dead and gone.

E.J. Wade: Excuse me, my father was born without full rights. You also have a September 11th, victim compensation fund and those people are no longer here.

Congresswoman Walters: They were killed by terrorist!

E.J. Wade: Who killed us? Did black people get lynched by imaginary gummi bears? Terrorist! This was terrorism against citizens on U.S. soil!

(The crowd goes wild as the head of the committee bangs the gavel)

E.J. Wade: Families of victims of the Holocaust also get compensation as standing in the shoes of their ancestors not to mention our tax dollars going to Israel every year.

Congresswoman Walters: We just don't have the money. So many Americans will be against this!

E.J. Wade: Many Americans were against the bail out of Wall Street to the tune of 4 trillion.

Congresswoman Walters: Let's say you and the others somehow magically vote me out. That still does not grant you damages.

E.J. Wade: We are about 14 percent of America but I am sure there are pissed off white people too who are tired to seeing what happened to us get spread out to benefit all these other groups. For example, people tried to coin the term Juan Crow to push back for illegal immigration. You have people pushing for open borders and many Americans are against that and the language used was stolen from our struggle. I am willing to bet it will save all tax payers money if you cut out all of these other people who were not Jim Crowed and enslaved. You will no longer be able to attach everybody on Earth to the enslavement and mistreatment to black Americans. You already spend the money, you just keep it away from us. You spend 30,000 per year to lock up a black man but won't give him 30,000 to start a business but during the Homestead act gave thousands of acres to white people for simply being white.

Congresswoman Walters: Other groups have suffered mistreatment and discrimination

E.J. Wade: They have to make their own justice claims for now on. Why should we fight for those who undermine us? We will start looking into these budgets and see what goes where.

Congresswoman Walters: Thank you for this testimony and we will take it under consideration.

E.J. Wade: Don't ask Black Americans, Descendants of Jim Crow for any support on any matters until our claim is met.

(The congresswoman and congressman step away from their mics)

Congressman Mitch: They're asking for a lot

Congresswoman Walters: Not really… We have sent more money to other countries for less. Maybe we should just make them full Americans and be done with this.

Congressman Mitch: Many white people and other groups won't like it

Congresswoman Walters: I'm sure they didn't like not having rights or dignity for 88 years as citizens. It is harder to deny claims of citizens when we take their rights and lives away. As slaves they were not citizens and slavery was legal. This argument is different. America stole lives and money from citizens. Our country is only as good as our personnel. We let white citizens be God over Black citizens. We can delay this but this claim is valid. Don't you see what they just did? Every other group highlights slavery and they skip over

Jim Crow in 10 seconds. This bastard has wrapped himself in Jim Crow because all of those laws violated some Amendment to the Constitution.

Congressman Mitch: 88 years at 100 billion! He is talking almost 9 trillion dollars.

Congresswoman Walters: It can be intergenerational not all at once. We sneeze trillions. We print the fucking money.

Congressman Mitch: And if I say no and tell them go to hell?

Congresswoman Walters: Be prepared for a long fight. We can't just say "well nobody walking around today owned slaves", 15 members met and shook hands and agreed to take the rights of millions.

(The congressman and woman walk back over and have seat. They both drink their water silently)

Congressman Mitch: I have one more question. I was told your ancestor was famous. Who was he…

E.J. Wade: Theo Wade. He wrote memoirs after surviving journeys with Mercy Justice. Mercy died but his wife Sue was pregnant. Theo Wade also married a woman named Abbie. Abbie attended Howard University. You murdered thousands after enslaving millions sir. The woman to my right is Sue Justice. She is the "Great Great" Granddaughter of Mercy Justice and Sue.

The congress look at the young lady standing next to E.J. She didn't say a word. She just stared back with an intense look on her face. Her presents made the hairs on the back of peoples necks stand up. It was clear, the spirit of Mercy lived within her.

1877 Flashback

Holly Springs Mississippi

Badger: Come here little girl!

Ida B. Wells: Sir

Badger: Did you steal that candy?

Ida B. Wells: I have never stolen anything in my life sir.

Badger: I am kidding. You don't have to fear me. Go, run along now little girl. Go on now, get!

The girl stares at Badger with no fear in her eyes. She doesn't flinch or move at all. Badger stares back at the young girl. He smiles and then walks out of the store. Badger felt a feeling of dread come over him. There was something going on with that little girl. Badger heads to South Carolina and is eventually killed by Mercy Justice and his team of heroes.

Ida B. Wells was born a slave but the Emancipation Proclamation freed her in 1863. President Lincoln under the pressure of the Radical Republicans Emancipated 3.5 million African people who had been enslaved with the first ship arriving in 1619. Slavery had been outlawed on the high seas leaving the only option for southern whites to rely only on breeding and enslaving the children of the enslaved. The North would often purchase domestic help from southern plantations. Once freed, Ida B. Wells went to school with her mother during a time where newly freed black citizens were rushing to get educated.

1878

Doctor: Excuse me, I apologize ma'am, but your father didn't make it. Mr. Wells is dead.

Ida B. Wells: Can you please give me a minute? Just go...

Doctor: I am sorry.

(A man with a top hat approaches)

Top hat: James was a good man. He was part of our fraternal order. It is now our responsibility to take care of his remaining children. I'm sorry my dear. Yellow fever respects nobody.

Ida B. Wells: You're not splitting us up! I will take care of them.

Top hat: Please, we wish to help.

Ida B. Wells: This is my family, this is my responsibility.

Top hat: Very well, we have to take his case with us. He wished for us to have it.

Ida signals for the men to take it. Elizabeth "Izzy Bell" Warrenton and James Wells along with one of her siblings had passed away from yellow fever. Ida B. Wells took over the task of taking care of her remaining siblings.

Ida decides it is up to her to take care of her siblings and not split the family up. She makes herself look older and becomes a teacher in order to take care of her family.

1884

Fanny: Look at you, you look so smart. Your grandmother would be proud.

Ida B. Wells: Well, we have to work hard now. No excuses, got to pull ourselves up by the bootstraps and make something of ourselves.

Fanny: Well, you just be careful out there. We might be a large population in Memphis but the whites still control Tennessee.

Ida B. Wells: Well I'm an American citizen now. It's my right to go and contribute.

(Fanny gives Ida a look and keeps cooking. Ida heads out to catch the train.)

White lady on train: Excuse me sir… Sir

Train worker 1: Yes ma'am, how can I help you?

White lady on train: Is this the lady's cart?

Train worker 1: Why yes it is

White lady on train: Is this the lady's cart? Speak up.

Train worker 1: Yes.

White lady on train: Why is that nigger girl allowed to sit here?

Train worker 1: I am so sorry. We will have her move at once.

(Train worker one approaches Ida B. Wells.)

Train worker 1: Ma'am we need you to move to the smoker's cart.

Ida B. Wells: I paid for a ticket to sit here. My ticket just as good as anybody else.

Train worker 1: People are complaining.

Ida B. Wells: They can always walk. They don't have to ride the train if they don't want to ride with Negroes.

(The white lady gasp)

Train worker 2: Enough, move at once. You get your uppity behind up or I'll grab you up!

Ida B. Wells: And if you grab me I'm going to bite you.

Train worker 2: She just said she would bite me.

Ida B. Wells: I suggest you keep your hands to yourself. I have done nothing wrong. I have broken no laws.

Train worker 1: Just grab her, she won't bite you.

Ida B. Wells: Don't you grab me!

(The train worker grabs Ida and is bitten on the hand)

Train worker 1: Ouch! She bit me! The crazy nigger bit me!

Train worker 2: Have you lost your mind nigger?

(The two men grab Ida and rough her up as they pull her out of the train cart. She attempts to stay seated so the men get rough with her.)

Ida B. Wells: I paid for my seat!

Train worker 1: You shut your mouth.

(The men pull Ida out of the lady's cart as the white women and others on the train clap and cheer.)

Ida B Wells goes on to sue the Train Company for 500.00 and wins but the decision is overturned by a crooked appellate court. Ida has dinner with a few of her male and female co-workers

Mary: Did you really bite somebody.

Ida B. Wells: That's nothing more than an ugly rumor…

(Chase gives Ida a look)

Ida B. Wells: I bit that cracker so hard

Mary: I'm going to buy you a drink.

Adelia: You're so brave. I would have been scared.

Ida B. Wells: Should we not be equal since we are citizens now?

Mary: I don't know if we are really citizens.

Ida B. Wells: According to the 14th Amendment we are citizens.

Mary: The constitution don't work for Negroes. Look how good the 13th Amendment is working. They rounded up a group of Negro men and made them work for free yesterday.

Ida B. Wells: How can that be possible, they must have done something wrong to just get snatched up like that.

Mary: Did you?

Ida B. Wells: No.

Adelia: Right and wrong depends on the color of your skin. If you're white then you're right.

Ida B. Wells: That's the dumbest thing I have ever heard.

Mary: Nothing changed. They just made the plantation bigger. I don't know when you are going to learn that the only real citizens in America are white people.

(Ida silently finished her food as she looks down at her plate.)

Ida B. Wells: I was certain the law would protect my rights. I won and they took my victory back.

Adelia: They have to set a legal precedent to let whites know that nobody will help us.

Ida B. Wells: What about the Republicans?

Mary: Nobody is going to help Negroes.

Ida B. Wells: I wish I could just gather my race up and fly away.

Mary: The white man kills birds too.

Ida B. Wells: I was thinking more of an Angel

Mary: Negro labor built everything and now we are locked out. I'm still a slave.

Adelia: What are you going to do now?

Ida B. Wells: I'm going to start writing. I'm not going to sit silent and let evil win.

Adelia: But you're so good at teaching

Ida B. Wells: I'm going to teach America.

(Chase gives Ida a look)

Mary: I think you will need a pen name.

Adelia: Moses!

Ida B. Wells: I think Moses is taken. I was thinking Iola.

Adelia: I love it.

The End

Credits roll as we quote reporters and political pundits

"It does get into this interesting area of where we are as a country about identity what does it mean to be black" Who is black and who isn't"

Alexandria Ocasio Cortez

South By Southwest Conference SXSW 2019

"What do you do with for example Barack Obama whose father was black and not from the United States therefore not having history with slavery and a mother who is white. Would his family receive slavery reparations?"

"Those who were harmed from Jim Crow I think that would be an easier case, but again it's going to be hard to determine who pays"

"Ben Shapiro"

Fox News 2019

"I don't think reparations for something that happened 150 years ago, for whom none of us currently living are responsible is a good idea."

"Mitch McConnell"

CNN News 2019

"I'm not going to sit here and say I am going to do something that's only going to benefit black people, Noooo!

Kamala Harris

The Grio 2019

"Can.. Can I get some water,I really did need a glass of water, this is not a stunt."

President Barack Obama 2016

Flint Water crises CBS News

"What have we done to immigrants? We owe black people something, immigrants haven't even been in this country".

"That's why the Democrats are dropping the blacks and moving on to the Hispanics"

Ann Coulter

ABC News 2012

"What's your message to black kids, to people of color, that their biggest contribution to justice and self fulfilment is to parade around with a chip on their shoulder like a victim?"

"And Colin, Who's getting away with murder? I'd like to see some evidence to back that up because that is a pretty strong claim.

"When will those in black communities take a step back and take some "response a damn bility" for the problems in black communities because it seems to me blaming white people for all of your problems might make you the racist"

Tomi Lahren 2016

The Blaze

"Reporter: "You tweeted about Black Lives Matter, Meet the New KKK. Which you later deleted, do you regret writing that?

I deleted it, listen I know there's people that are going to disagree with some of the things that I say and that's ok. I'm not here to please everyone."

"Something has been scripped from me, that's my ability to work, my ability to have a voice. "

Tomi Lahren 2017

ABC News

"There are those who contend that it does not benefit African-Americans to get them into the University of Texas where they do not do well, as opposed to having them go – a less advanced school, a less..uh slower-track school where they do well.

Justice Antonin Scalia

2015 Fisher V. University of Texas

"Jesus was a white man too, but you know.. it's like he

was a historical figure that was a verifiable fact"

Megyn Kelly

Fox News 2013

"Uncle Luke is no political Master Mind or Strategist Why do black men keep popping up with their unsolicited opinions about Kamala Harris"?

Simone D. Sanders

Twitter 2019

"Reporter: A lot African Americans are starting to call for reparations for the many years of stolen labor through slavery is that something that you would support as president

Bernie Sanders: No, I don't think so, I mean first of all it's likelihood of getting through a congress is …second of all I think it would be very divisive

Bernie Sanders, Fusion 2016

"Guys don't ever forget that Immigrants built the United States of America"

Pit Bull, Cuban pop artist

Latin American Music Awards 2017

"African-Americans built this nation, and you're just starting to get real credit for that, we all built it, but you were such a massive part of it, bigger than you were given credit for, does that make since"

President Trump

Young Black Leadership Summit 2019

"If you get raped by a pack of niggers it will be your fault".

Mel Gibson 2010 audio leak

"You have a black president, you have the heads of almost every department in this government of African-American heritage, that's still not enough"?

"What about the Africans who have come here since slave times and have benefited from the works of the Africans who were enslaved, should the African Immigrants also be forced to pay reparations"

"Look sir, you're dealing with a man with a PhD. And has written 28 books you're out of your league"

Michael Savage

Savage Nation 2017

"This is one country, it has become one country because all of us, and all the people who came here had an equal chance to develop their talents. We cannot say that 10 percent of the population that you can't have that right. That your children can't have the chance to develop whatever talents they have, that the only way that they are going to get their rights is to go in the street and demonstrate.

I think we owe them and we owe ourselves a better country than that, therefore I am asking for your help and making it easier for us to move ahead and provide the kind of equality of treatment which we would want for ourselves."

John F. Kennedy 1963

Assassinated November 22, 1963

It is believed that the modern commission of 1876 still meets today.

BONUS: THE BLACK WEALTH APPARATUS

A few generations ago a man named Eddie Wade married a woman named Lillie Saterio Wade. They did not have full rights or opportunity because of their skin color. That generation like generations before had to participate in a hard fight to simply have the right to breathe air, eat food, work, or even walk down the street. One of their sons was named Bruce. His generation also did not have full rights as citizens, not even on paper. He was spit on and attacked by white Americans while trying to get an education. Bruce still received a college education at Florida Memorial University and went on to have children as well. One of his sons was given the nickname of E.J. the youngest son of Rev. Wade. I am E.J. the first born in a long line of Wades to have full rights on paper my entire life. The mission given to me from the creator was to create the blueprint that would later become The Black Wealth Apparatus. The Black Wealth Apparatus is the beginning of correcting what was done to African people enslaved in America. The United States Government refused to officially go on record and correct the enslavement of black people. The United States In 1988 under President Ronald Regan gave an official apology and paid 20,000 dollars to every Japanese person held in internment camps. Black American (DOS) didn't get one red cent.

Black Americans (DOS) are now having a difficult time competing economically because every other group was given a head start or helping hand by the U.S. government. Black Americans (DOS) were told voting Democrat was the way, failing to realize (soft racist) who call themselves liberal or progressive were involved in two different compromises. The first was the compromise for Africans to be classified as 3/5 human and another compromise to withdraw troops after the Civil War and allow the Jim Crow era and Black codes. We will not find the answer in liberals and Democrats (or Republicans) but instead let us make our primary focus a black economic base.

I started with a paper called the Black Print which became The Black Wealth Apparatus blueprint. I was met with resistance by so called black leaders who were more concerned with who would get the credit. I didn't give up. I kept going because I understand what is upon us. As demographics shift they will create an apartheid state. To continue to put the lives of black people into the hands of others is criminal.

Staff

The Grand Council of the Black Wealth Apparatus will be made up of 10 staff members. Out of those 10 staff members 5 will be the decision making body. They will interview candidates for grants from the Black Wealth Apparatus. They will review business plans as well as interview the people. They will decide where we will get the most impact for our money and distribute all of the money to the people with the exception of 10 percent to pay the staff. The panel of 5 is designed to be able to vote with a majority of 3 for major decisions. The staff members must be black/ African Americans who are descendants of slavery in North America. The staff may not hold a position as an elected official at any level of government.

The second set of 5 are intelligence staff. The job of the intelligence staff will be to keep everybody honest. If someone scams the Council by taking money for a business grant and instead uses it for anything other than business it is up to intelligence staff to hire the attorney and oversee the lawsuit to recover those funds. The intelligence staff will also watch the decision making staff to make sure they are not involved in any type of scams that would put the Black Wealth Apparatus in jeopardy.

The 10 percent will be used to pay the staff and the bank. A black owned bank must hold the funds. The black owned bank must keep records anytime funds are taken out. One of the 5 intelligence members will be a records keeper. They shall record who received the funds and what they did with the funds. The Grand Council of the Black Wealth Apparatus shall meet monthly to distribute funds to one of the 48 cities.

Contractors who do not work full time may also be paid out of the 10 percent. We will have to pay law firms, IT personnel and other positions that are required for a well running group that is not over staffed. A staff member may only apply for a grant once they have left the seat of that position. Staff members may not be lifetime staffers, they must vacate the position after a term of 4 years unless they decide to step down before that time. A staff member who has not served an entire 4 year term may apply and if approved they may return to finish their 4 years.

Qualifications for a staff position should include something verifiable that they have done in their background. A college degree, business ownership, has held a political office in the past, has served in the military etc. We don't need to be elitist or say you must have a college degree or you must have been a politician, but we also don't want to hand the keys over to someone who may need to get a little bit of real world experience before dealing with such a high profile and stressful position.

I am all for criminal justice reform and even for rehabilitation. At the same time if a person has been convicted of theft or robbery it would not be wise to put them in charge of millions of dollars of a vulnerable community. It would also not be wise to place any men or women into leadership who have been found guilty of sexual assault or sex crimes. It would also not be a good idea to have a council of all men or all women for that matter.

Staff may be reimbursed or payed for travel dealing in matters of The Black Wealth Apparatus. Staff may be reimbursed for meals while conducting business for The Black Wealth Apparatus. Staff may be reimbursed for classes that they took to better help them develop and run the Council. (For classes taken during the time of them serving).

Funding

The funds from the Black Wealth Apparatus will be raised by and from African-Americans / Black Americans who are descendants of slavery in North America. Everyone is encouraged to pay 1.00 per month. How did I come up with 1.00 per month? It was the lowest number I could think of that would not hurt the pockets of any person. I was still met with resistance and grumbling from a few black men which was surprising. The excuse for not wanting to provide 1.00 per month was "he wanted a return on his investment". Here is my response to those people. If you do not donate 1.00 per month to the Black Wealth Apparatus you will not qualify for a grant. There should be a database that shows who paid and how long they have paid. If someone decided to pay 1.00 a month (for only one month) before we come to their city and never supported it before that information should be made available. The only thing that will not count in the decision is the amount of the money they donated. (on a monthly basis) If a person who has decided to give 100.00 per month instead of 1.00 per month for example they will be treated the same as the person who have faithfully paid that 1.00. We don't want people to use money to influence the decisions of the council. The minimum is 1.00 per month. Before the actual creation of the Black Wealth Apparatus all we need is a verbal pledge. We don't want strange crooks going around collecting money on our behalf and then the money vanishes. We need an official site for collecting money. This book will be the official ritual. All others are unauthorized and fraudulent.

In America we have roughly 43 million African-Americans. If you subtract the children we should still be able to collect about 30 million dollars per month as the base amount. On top of the base amount people who have more and want to donate more should. No pressure, no passing the collection plate back around, but if a black millionaire decided to donate 10,000 that would help to replace what children can't donate. If we have any real white allies, we encourage them to donate. As a matter of fact if you refuse to give 1.00 per month to the Black Wealth Apparatus how can you be an ally? Any Black person and any white ally who are adults and refuse to pay 1.00 we should be looking at them as not for the black community. We should deem them to be enemies of the black community. People like Tim Wise and all of these white liberal scholars it is time to pay up. We can go from a base number of 30 million to 60 million.

Imagine if in a random month like July we poured 60 million into New York. (subtract 10 percent to run the Apparatus and pay the staff) That would be 54 million dollars going directly into the hands of black Americans for job creation. Now the next month we hit Houston and then Atlanta, and then Charlotte, and then Miami. We keep going into we hit 48 main cities. We will see a huge drop in black unemployment and poverty in 1 year. To hit 48 cities it would take 4 years and then we double back and hit those 48 cites again and then again! We will have 48 Atlanta's. Even if you don't get a grant yourself you or your kids or family members will have jobs.

I listened to a very bright man speak. His name is Dr. Claude Anderson. He talked about how on several occasions he almost built Africa towns and then black politicians would turn the idea down. He also stated at one point in time minority funding was placed in Miami and it some way, some how, went to Cubans and not black people. (all of it) The information he provided left me with more questions than answers. How can we avoid mistakes of the past. (The Freedman's Bank) We simply come together as Black Americans (DOS) raise the money which is totally legal and requires no permission from politicians and then we do it ourselves. It does not cancel out black people who want to continue to ask for reparations (WE SHOULD ALSO GET REPARATIONS) it creates a base to grow from...

It is criminal to continue to place the lives of black people into anyone else's hands

48 cities

1. Atlanta Ga

2. Akron Oh

3. Baton Rogue LA

4. Baltimore MD

5. Birmingham AL

6. Boston MA

7. Chicago IL

8. Charlotte NC

9. Columbus OH

10. Cincinnati OH

11. Columbia SC

12. Cleveland OH

13. Detroit MI

14. Dallas TX

15. Durham NC

16. Flint MI

17. Ft. Lauderdale FL

18. Greensboro NC

19. Houston TX

20. Indianapolis / Gary IN

21. Jackson MS

22. Jacksonville FL

23. Jersey City NJ

24. Kansa MO

25. Los Angeles

26. Lafayette LA

27. Little Rock AR

28. Miami FL

29. Memphis TN

30. Milwakee WI

31. Norfolk VA

32. Newport News VA

33. Newark NJ

34. New York NY

35. New Orleans LA

36. Orlando FL

37. Oakland FL

38. Philadelphia PA

39. Raleigh NC

40. Richmond CA

41. Sacramento CA

42. San Antonio TX

43. Seattle WA

44. San Diego CA

45. Vallejo CA

46. West Palm Beach FL

47. Washington DC

48. ?

? City 48 will be decided by the council.

If you do not live in one of these cities or surrounding areas you are welcome to relocate and open a business in that city if you are selected.

Eligibility

In order to be eligible you must be classified as black/ African American descendants of slavery in North America. The people who are eligible are a unique group to America. People who have a connection to the start of America. The people who actually built America. We are in a unique position to challenge systemic racism and white supremacy because we have been dealing with it the longest. We are also in a unique position because our struggle in the Civil Rights era opened the flood gates for immigration in America.

If someone is using false information in order to fake eligibility that would be considered fraud and that person would be held liable. African-Americans/ black

Americans who are descendants of slavery in North America are also the only group that have been refused reparations. The Colonies and the United States paid reparations in the form of freedom dues to those classified as white. The United States also paid reparations to slave owners who had to give up their "property". The United States allowed sexual assault to be inflicted upon African men and women. The Unites States allowed people's children to be taken away from them and then sold off as animals.

Black Americans/ African Americans descendants of slavery in North America also have a constitutional relationship with the United States. Article one section two of the constitution referred to black people as 3/5 persons. A compromise made when liberals did not want us counted as people at all because of the voting power it would have given white owners. In 1877 another compromise was made to remove U.S. Troops from the South and allow thousands of black people to be lynched over time. They allowed the formation of the KKK to put a stop to black voting rights and ended reconstruction after 12 years referring to black people as receiving special treatment.

Many African people who migrated to North America prior to slavery were also reclassified from Native American to Negro. They were cheated out of all of the treaties that stated that former slaves who are now free men were supposed to get some of the resources from those treaties. Federal law enforcement also admitted to keeping tabs on Civil Rights leaders who were peaceful like Dr. Martin Luther King Jr. The Serviceman's Readjustment Act of 1944 also excluded black veteran's benefits including the G.I. Bill after World War 2. The United States built the white middle class and legally denied black people the same rights.

Members of what was referred to as the Five Civilized Tribes participated in the enslavement of African people. The Cherokee, Creek, and Seminole Indians have been documented in denying those Africans part of the benefits under those treaties. It has also been documented that people who are classified as white were able to add their names to the Dawes Rolls and get the benefits denied to black Americans. My father's Great Grandmother was full blooded Cherokee which is where the name Saterio (Satara) comes from in my family tree.

No other groups who migrated to America have gone through what black American (DOS) have gone though. It is for this reason only African / Black Americans (DOS) are allowed to apply for grants under the Black Wealth Apparatus. The religion of the candidate does not matter. The sexual orientation of the candidate does not matter. The political leanings of the candidate does not matter. The gender of the candidate does not matter. I also exclude myself from being able to receive a grant but will donate. This is a once in a lifetime grant per person selected.

Accountability

Accountability is the most important section. If African Americans / black Americans (DOS) participate and if our allies who are classified as white participate we cannot fail. The only way we fail is if we don't hold people accountable who we hand the keys to the kingdom. This is the first time in decades that we have a chance to fix our collective situation. This is the first time in decades people are not able to pull a "sleight of hand trick". Affirmative Action was designed to be corrective action for those who were enslaved but studies show black males benefit the least from it.

The chosen 10 to have access to the Black Wealth Apparatus will have checks and balances and answer to the people. We will have one official Black Wealth Apparatus. Any imitations who attempt to use the name will be called out. The 10 main staff members will be transparent with the bank and the bank will be transparent to the people. The intelligence body will keep the decision making body honest. We will deal with people who aim to sabotage from within by any means necessary. Nobody will have a term that exceeds 4 years and the people can invoke a vote of no confidence if members become corrupt. 90 percent of the money raised will go towards the people and will be accounted for.

The decision making body will have the ability to cast a vote 3/5 majority to symbolize America classifying us as 3/5 persons, they will have the power to remove anyone for proven corruption. The Intelligence body will also have the power 3/5 votes to remove any member for proven corruption. Attorneys may be paid out of the 10 percent and if necessary Attorney's may be paid out of the 90 percent if the 10 percent is not enough to ensure we have legal representation and the ability to stop fraud. There shall be a fail-safe in place to prevent anyone or anybody from withdrawal of all of the funds.

Before any member is installed in the position they will submit to a background check. They will present their spouse if they are married as well. The original 10 will be installed by the people and the members to follow will also be installed by the people. There shall be a mirror group of 10 back-ups who will never be in the same location as the 10 members. The back-ups shall not receive pay unless activated and may not be activated unless the main members pass away or vacate the seat. The primary job of the back-up members is to step in if something happens to the main members. The back-up members must be African American / black Americans descendants of slavery in North America. The back-up members are to be installed by the people but kept away from media and other areas of "spotlight", after installed they shall quietly go about their everyday lives.

The intelligence members will have the task of making sure the people who receive the funds use the funds for a business. They will check to make sure the business plan is actually being followed and that the people use the grant and not abuse the grant. If a candidate who receives a grant is discovered to have misused the grant the body of 10 may take whatever means necessary to correct that action. The body will have the right to do background research to make sure candidates are not dishonest when it comes to their application and submission. An agreement must be signed to use the grant for intended purposes. This is the only authorized ritual and shall remain affordable to the people. The ritual shall be updated as needed.

Urgent Needs and Exclusions

The decision making body shall have the right to take it into consideration if a particular business will have a high chance of success and employ other black people. A black law firm that employs 10 people may be weighted higher than one individual who wants to sell bicycles. One business may only need 80,000 dollars while another business may need 400,000 dollars. The Council of the Black Wealth Apparatus may not choose (ever) 1 person to give all of the funds to. If a community has certain needs for example a daycare the decision making body may take that into consideration. The funds are not first come first serve. The funds will go to those who have taken the time to draft a serious business plan.

When meeting and choosing candidates the Council of the Black Wealth Apparatus will always give the first grant to a black woman. We will never stop any gender from receiving the funds, but the very first person each month in each city shall be a black/African American woman (DOS). She was sexually assaulted and told that she never ever can be first. It will be our pleasure to choose a black woman first and then the other candidates may come forward, men and women to receive the funds. Along with her approval that black woman/ African American woman will receive a symbolic crown. The first male will receive a symbolic hammer as a builder. We shall call this the opening ceremony of the Crown and Hammer.

The Black Wealth Apparatus shall never provide funds to a religious body. The Black Wealth Apparatus will never provide funds for a strip club / topless bar. The Black

Wealth Apparatus will never provide funds to a recording label for the purposes of making music or to an individual recording artist. We don't have any problem with the groups we just named. We simply wish to avoid oversaturation in the market. I will never be eligible for a grant. I remove myself from eligibility to receive a grant.

The Black Wealth Apparatus excludes anyone who is not a black American / African American descendants of slavery in North America. We do not encourage business owners to discriminate in their hiring practices. We do reserve the right to meet the needs of those enslaved in America with grants. We will not deny a spot on the council or a grant to someone due to gender or sexual orientation. We will not deny someone a spot on the council or a grant due to their religious background. There is only one official Black Wealth Apparatus. All others are fraudulent and the ritual shall remain affordable to the people.

America:

We do not take a political stance (as far as which party you must vote for). We do not take a religious stance. We do however, choose to be Americans and we choose to cloak ourselves in the American flag and to be part of America as Foundational Black Americans. We are not anti-American. We just wish to see the Constitution followed. Either The Constitution means something or it does not. People who succeeded from America claim to love the constitution, but do they really if they were ready to give up being American just to be able to own and subjugate African people? The rebel flag is a traitor's flag. The people who wear and carry it are traitors to America. We simply want and need our piece of America since we built it. We have fought in every war and we have never attempted to attack or overthrow or succeed from America. We are the most patriotic Americans ever. Let us be clear what this is about. Many people simply wish to not see black Americans as citizens. It is the reason they killed President Lincoln and the reason they killed President Kennedy. It is the reason they held the commission of 1876 and gave up an election. It is the reason the KKK is allowed to exist (no other terrorist group has been allowed to walk around except the KKK). People are angry, because we have a direct relationship with the 14th Amendment to the constitution. Be proud to be American and stop walking away from what we built. Stop allowing people to come here illegally and unlawfully. Step into your earned place. We will stop using language asking people to treat us right, instead let us ask crooked government officials why they are breaking the law.

God bless you all

The Free Will Rise Again!

M.O.S.H. Museum of Science and History. The stacks of money represent the wealth of the white, African-American, Latino and Asian community.

The University of Missouri have a display in their law school dedicated to Lloyd L. Gaines. Mr. Gaines was denied admission to the University of Missouri School of Law because of his race. After the Supreme Court ruled in his favor the General Assembly established the Lincoln University School of Law in 1939. Lloyd L. Gaines "mysteriously disappeared" after his victory.

Convict Leasing 1903. Little Children leased out for work during the era of Jim Crow

Roger Williams University in Nashville, TN, 1899

In Memory of

John G. Jones, Chicago Illinois, Founder of the Prince Hall Shriners.

In 1881 John G. Jones was admitted to the Illinois Bar. He fought hard for Civil Rights.

The Prince Hall Shriners won "the great litigation" which took from 1914 to 1929. The AAONMS vs. AEAONMS

R.I.P. Reginald Fields DDGHP HRAM

REPORTING LIVE FROM JIM CROW

Ida B. Wells

1877

E.J. Wade

ACT 1

1877

Holly Springs Mississippi

Badger: Come here little girl!

Ida B. Wells: Sir

Badger: Did you steal that candy?

Ida B. Wells: I have never stolen anything in my life sir.

Badger: I'm kidding. You don't have to fear me. Go, run along now little girl. Go on now, get!

The girl stares at Badger with no fear in her eyes. She doesn't flinch or move at all. Badger stares back at the young girl. He smiles and then walks out of the store. Badger felt a feeling of dread come over him. There was something going on with that little girl. Badger heads to South Carolina and is eventually killed by Mercy Justice and his team of heroes.

Ida B. Wells was born a slave but the Emancipation Proclamation freed her in 1863. President Lincoln, under the pressure of the Radical Republicans Emancipated 3.5

million African people who had been enslaved with the first ship arriving in 1619. Slavery had been outlawed on the high seas, the only option southern whites had left was to breed their slaves and enslave the children. The North would often purchase domestic help from southern plantations. Once freed, Ida B. Wells went to school with her mother during a time where newly freed black citizens were rushing to get educated.

[1877 becomes one of the most significant dates to African-Americans whether we know it or not. It was the date when it was decided behind closed doors that black Americans would become 2nd class citizens. A long battle between Republicans and Democrats lead them to reach a compromise. The compromise came with promises such as help with the economy but among all, it came with an agreement that the Supreme Court, The Office of the President, and Congress would turn away while the south dealt with African-Americans however they saw fit. The battle had gotten so fierce that Democrats started using the term "Tilden or Blood", meaning they would seek out a violent solution if they lost the election. The electoral votes for Florida, Louisiana, and South Carolina would be traded for lives of every newly freed black American.]

1878

Doctor: Excuse me, I apologize ma'am, but your father didn't make it. Mr. Wells is dead.

Ida B. Wells: Can you please give me a minute? Just go…

Doctor: I am sorry.

(A man with a top hat approaches)

Top hat: James was a good man. He was part of our fraternal order. It is now our responsibility to take care of his remaining children. I'm sorry my dear. Yellow fever respects nobody.

Ida B. Wells: You're not splitting us up! I will take care of them.

Top hat: Please, we wish to help.

Ida B. Wells: This is my family, this is my responsibility.

Top hat: Very well, we have to take his case with us. He wished for us to have it.

Ida signals for the men to take it. Elizabeth "Izzy Bell" Warrenton and James Wells along with one of her siblings had passed away from Yellow Fever. Ida B. Wells took over the task of taking care of her remaining siblings. Ida decides it is up to her to take care of her siblings and not split the family up. She makes herself look older and becomes a teacher in order to take care of her family.

1884

Fanny: Look at you, you look so smart. Your grandmother would be proud.

Ida B. Wells: Well, we have to work hard now. No excuses, got to pull ourselves up by the bootstraps and make something of ourselves.

Fanny: Well, you just be careful out there. We might be a large population in Memphis but the whites still control Tennessee.

Ida B. Wells: Well I'm an American citizen now. It's my right to go and contribute.

(Fanny gives Ida a look and keeps cooking. Ida heads out to catch the train.)

[At this point in time, the wisdom of her older Ant kicks in, she knows that they will be dealing with the same racism and evil but she decides not to "burst the bubble" of young Ida. Young Ida B. Wells grew up in the Victorian age and was considered a "pretty girl" or a "girly girl" to an extent. She accepted a new ideology that as citizens it was up to black Americans to pull ourselves up by our boot straps]

White lady on train: Excuse me sir… Sir

Train worker 1: Yes ma'am, how can I help you?

White lady on train: Is this the lady's cart?

Train worker 1: Why yes it is

White lady on train: Is this the lady's cart? Speak up.

Train worker 1: Yes.

White lady on train: Why is that nigger girl allowed to sit here?

Train worker 1: I am so sorry. We will have her move at once.

(Train worker one approaches Ida B. Wells.)

Train worker 1: Ma'am we need you to move to the smoker's cart.

Ida B. Wells: I paid for a ticket to sit here. My ticket just as good as anybody else.

Train worker 1: People are complaining.

Ida B. Wells: They can always walk. They don't have to ride the train if they don't want to ride with Negroes.

(The white lady gasp)

Train worker 2: Enough, move at once. You get your uppity behind up or I'll grab you up!

Ida B. Wells: And if you grab me I'm going to bite you.

Train worker 2: She just said she would bite me.

Ida B. Wells: I suggest you keep your hands to yourself. I have done nothing wrong. I have broken no laws.

Train worker 1: Just grab her, she won't bite you.

Ida B. Wells: Don't you grab me!

(The train worker grabs Ida and is bitten on the hand)

Train worker 1: Ouch! She bit me! The crazy nigger bit me!

Train worker 2: Have you lost your mind nigger?

(The two men grab Ida and rough her up as they pull her out of the train cart. She attempts to stay seated so the men get rough with her.)

Ida B. Wells: I paid for my seat!

Train worker 1: You shut your mouth.

(The men pull Ida out of the lady's cart as the white women and others on the train clap and cheer.)

Ida B Wells goes on to sue the Train Company for 500.00 and wins but the decision is overturned by a crooked appellate court. Ida has dinner with a few of her male and female co-workers

Mary: Did you really bite somebody.

Ida B. Wells: That's nothing more than an ugly rumor…

(Mary gives Ida a look)

Ida B. Wells: I have rights too!

Mary: I'm going to buy you a drink.

Adelia: You're so brave. I would have been scared.

Ida B. Wells: Should we not be equal since we are citizens now?

Mary: I don't know if we are really citizens.

Ida B. Wells: According to the 14th Amendment we are citizens.

Mary: The constitution don't work for Negroes. Look how good the 13th Amendment is working. They rounded up a group of Negro men and made them work for free yesterday.

Ida B. Wells: How can that be possible, they must have done something wrong to just get snatched up like that.

Mary: Did you?

Ida B. Wells: No.

Adelia: Right and wrong, depends on the color of your skin. If you're white then you're right.

Ida B. Wells: That's the dumbest thing I have ever heard.

Mary: Nothing changed. They just made the plantation bigger. I don't know when you are going to learn that the only real citizens in America are white people.

(Ida silently finished her food as she looks down at her plate.)

Ida B. Wells: I was certain the law would protect my rights. I won and they took my victory back.

Adelia: They have to set a legal precedent to let whites know that nobody will help us.

Ida B. Wells: What about the Republicans?

Mary: Nobody is going to help Negroes.

Ida B. Wells: I wish I could just gather my race up and fly away.

Mary: The white man kills birds too.

Ida B. Wells: I was thinking more of an Angel

Mary: Negro labor built everything and now we are locked out. I'm still a slave.

Adelia: What are you going to do now?

Ida B. Wells: I'm going to start writing. I'm not going to sit silent and let evil win.

Adelia: But you're so good at teaching

Ida B. Wells: I'm going to teach America. The conditions are so poor at the school I teach at.

(Mary gives Ida a look)

Mary: I think you will need a pen name.

Adelia: Moses!

Ida B. Wells: I think Moses is taken. I was thinking Iola.

Adelia: I love it. (scene)

[Parts of the Civil Rights Act of 1875 had been struck down by Federal Courts leaving no real protection for Ida B. Wells. The attempt at passing the Civil Rights Act of 1875 angered many white Senators causing a revolt and giving them momentum for 1877]

Iola's Letter
Memphis Free Speech

Our time has come and we are not going to sit around and feel pity for ourselves. It is time to come together and improve our conditions as Negro Citizens in America. My mother went to school right next to me. She valued education. I have been described as a "princess" and a "Victorian" because I have found "the way" and I simply do not believe in Negroes sitting around and feeling sorry for ourselves. We pay taxes and our government has to work for us. This is supposed to be a government of the people according to the constitution. We want our just due and the same opportunity as others.

I reported the poor conditions of the school system in Memphis that Negro children attend. Education changed my life, I believe a proper education can be life changing for the Negro. I understand the white man carries blame for our condition but what should our response be? Look around, this country belongs to us too and so does the world. Open your eyes to education and to a beautiful world. I surround myself with friends who are hard workers. Smart and hard-working Negro men and women.

Iola

1892

Will Stewart: Our new store is finished

Calvin Mcdowell: It is beautiful.

Thomas Moss: All of our hard work. Look at it brothers. This is what I saw in my vision and now it is here.

Calvin Mcdowell: The People's Grocery

Will Stewart: Your little girl is going to be proud! She will say "look what my father built".

Thomas Moss: Thank you

(The neighboring store owner by the name of William Barrett looks over at the successful store owned by a coalition of successful Negro Businessmen.)

Posse Member 1: "Them" niggers are taking money from you William. You use to let the niggers go around back and buy from you. Did you forget we live in Shelby County?

William Barrett: Their actions are illegal. That store shouldn't even be there!

Posse Member 1: I say we walk over and give them a piece of our mind. They didn't ask for permission to put that store there.

William Barrett: Fucking uppity niggers. Let's go!

(William Barrett and Posse Member 1 approach the store)

Thomas Moss: How can I help you Mr. Barrett?

William Barrett: Hey boy, you done real good for yourself with this store. I don't recall you getting permission from me to open up a store here.

Thomas Moss: I didn't know I needed permission. We bought this land fair and square.

William Barrett: Don't you sassy me boy!

Thomas Moss: I apologize, I don't want any trouble.

Posse Member 1: We can always come back and shut your sassy mouth for you boy!

Will Stewart: I have to ask you two gentlemen to leave. This is our store.

Posse Member 1: I'll see you soon boy. You have a good day now.

(William Barrett picks up an apple and bites it. He drops it on the ground and walks out of the store)

Spring of 1892

Cornelius: My papa bought me those marbles. You're gonna let me win.

Armour: That's not how it works in "The Curve". If you lose then you lose.

Bobby: Well, our papa said you can't trust niggers.

Armour: Well I ain't no nigger. My papa told me I was made in the image of God!

Cornelius: God don't like no niggers.

Armour: Take it back!

Cornelius: No!

(The two boys grab each other and start to tussle. William Barrett watches from across the street and decided to join in on the argument. Cornelius's father was watching from a distance, he quickly ran up and struck Armour)

William Barrett: Hey, that little nigger touched a white boy! This is getting out of hand.

Will Stewart: Now Mr. Barrett, I told you to stop coming over here causing trouble sir.

Posse Member 1 runs over to the People's Grocery store and slaps one of the black men standing outside. A fight breaks out and men start fighting from both sides. William Barrett takes off running like a coward, leaving the remaining white men behind to get beaten down. He hides behind a building and peeks around the corner to make sure nobody noticed him. The young white boy who was playing marbles saw everything. He stares at William Barret with shame in his eyes. (Not being old enough to understand shame.) The anger grows inside of William Barret. He clinches his fist and then walks away.

William Barrett stops by the local Sheriff's office and slams the door behind him…

William Barrett: Dammit Sheriff, you said you would help us! We looked like cowards out there!

Sheriff Lynch: What happened?

William Barrett: The niggers, they outnumbered us. There was only 3 of us and it was 100 of them. We fought them off as long as we could.

Sheriff Lynch: You don't look like 100 niggers beat on you.

William Barrett: Well they did! Do you want to get

reelected Sheriff? You don't seem to understand my situation. Damn Yankees should have never freed them. Innocent white folk being terrorized in our own country!

Sheriff Lynch: Whatever you need. We can't let criminals hurt our citizens.

William Barrett: Make us deputies... Me and a few good men.

Sheriff Lynch: Stand up so I can swear you in. (scene)

The White League Assembles

Jared T.: I heard when the niggers attacked you turned and ran. We can't have people out there making us look weak. Now is the time for the rightful owners of America to take our seat as the unapologetic head. If you can't handle these animals then I can't justify you being the head of Shelby County.

William Barrett: I know what to do, I will take care of it.

Jared T.: That will be all Willie. I don't expect I will see you back at the hall until you clean up your mess.

Judge Julius Dubose: I am tired of the trash in "The Curve". Why is the Klan still in hiding? I don't see Ulysees Grant in power...

Judge Lynch: I made old Willie a deputy. We're still strong in Tennessee.

Jared T: Let's show South Carolina how to properly deal with these traitors. Do you feel the power judge? I feel the power. My papa, he had a slave named Walt. Old Walt tried to talk back one day, he tried to sassy my papa. He slapped that nigger in the mouth so hard his teeth came flying out. Old Walt never gave my papa lip again. He slapped those big old lips.

Judge Julius Dubose: I don't need a lecture. (scene)

[In history, you often hear of the KKK, but there was another powerful group who called themselves The White League. They were every bit as ruthless as the KKK. Ulysees S. Grant had broken the backs of the KKK with the Enforcement Acts.]

Will Stewart receives a phone call at The People's Grocery.

Will Stewart: Hello…

Voice: You're all going to die you uppity nigger!

Will Stewart: Don't call here again!

Thomas Moss: Who was that?

Will Stewart: They're making threats.

White shopper: Excuse me sir.

William turns to the shopper…

Will Stewart: Yes

White Shopper: William Barrett is good friends with a judge. I heard he is going to attack your store sir. I always thought you was a good Christian man. I would leave town if I was you.

Thomas Moss: We not going nowhere! We have rights now! The Negro just can't keep running.

(Will Stewart waits for the shopper to exit…)

Will Stewart: What are we going to do? William Barrett has friends!

Thomas Moss: I have to go talk to a lawyer. Things can get bad and we can lose everything we built. (Scene)

Thomas and Will pace back and forth in an attorney's office while they wait.

Lawyer: Mr. Moss, your store is located just outside of the city limits. The Sheriff doesn't have to protect you. You can always protect yourselves. This is after all a free country.

Ida B. Wells and her aunt have a discussion as she helps prepare dinner.

Ida B.Wells: It seems as though whenever I mention our rights you roll those eyes.

Fanny: Ain't no white man about to respect the rights of no colored person.

Ida B. Wells: They have to, it's the law. It's up to us to make them follow the law. What good is a country if the people don't follow their own constitution?

Fanny: Listen, I'm just saying be careful. These people have been evil for a long time. So long that they got good at it. They don't care about no law. They don't even care about the law of God. Do you hear me?

Ida B. Wells: It's still up to us to make them follow the law. We will be respectable and educated and we will pull ourselves up by the boot straps.

Fanny: Sit, eat, the salad is getting cold.

Ida B. Wells: The salad is supposed to be… owe you mean shut up. OK… (scene)

Six white deputies head to The People's Grocery to arrest Will Stewart. They were recently deputized and in plain clothes.

Deputy Cole: Are you boys ready?

(One of the men is making a noose as Deputy Cole loads his gun)

Three men head to the front of the store and three men head to the back of the store. The men creep into the store wearing plain clothes with their fire arms.

Bam!

The Sheriff and his men are met with a hail of bullets as one of them hit the ground. Nat Trigg, a black postman tries to exit and runs into Deputy Cole. Nat Trigg shoots Deputy Cole in the face and exits the store. Calvin McDowell is pulled from behind the counter!

Sheriff Lynch: You are under arrest. Make one move and I'll blow your nigger head off!

(They take Calvin McDowell and other men into custody.)

The Sheriff and his men retreat into William Barrett's store across the street.

Sheriff Lynch: Help! Help! We just got attacked.

William Barrett: What happened?

Sheriff Lynch: We got attacked! Those animals attacked us!

William Barrett: They attacked our lawmen! How much longer do we have to wait to kill them all!

Sheriff Lynch: I want you to round up every able bodied white man you can find. I'm going to lock this criminal up and then I'll be headed back with my best men.

Sheriff Lynch returns to the curve with deputies as others go through the Negro part of town knocking on doors and slapping residents. With Calvin Mcdowell already in custody the Sheriff started knocking the black residents down until they also took Will Stewart and Thomas Moss into custody.

Thomas Moss: I don't even know if the shop is locked. They're going to blame everything on us. I doubt we will even get a fair trial.

Calvin Mcdowell: Maybe that lawyer we was talking to earlier will help us.

Will Stewart: I doubt it, They don't like Negroes making money in Shelby County!

Thomas Moss: My wife saw them take me. God willing, she let people know what's going on.

(Judge Dubose enters)

Judge Dubose: You boys have caused quite a stir in my county.

Will Stewart: Sir, if I could just explain, it was all a big misunderstanding.

Judge Dubose: You shut your mouths! I will see to it that justice is delivered.

March 7th 1892

(Outside commotion)

Charles Biggs: Men, attention!

Judge Dubose looks outside to see a fairly large militia armed with rifles. The black Tennessee rifle militia had arrived to make sure the men got fair treatment. When Betty Moss arrived to try to bring her husband some food the judge turned her away. He also begin to squash the petitions from the lawyers of the various men that had showed up to help. Judge Dubose did not back down and the black Tennessee rifle militia had only made him more angry and determined. One of the attorneys handed a letter to Charles Biggs, the leader of the black militia.

Charles Biggs: The letter states that both officers who were wounded will survive. This is no longer a murder case.

Judge Dubose: Fine, we will process them and give them their fair trial. The men's family members can come back and see them in a couple of days.

Charles Biggs calls the black Tennessee rifle militia to attention. The men pack up and head out as things finally cool off.

[In the late 1800s you had a few rifle clubs or "black militia" forming. In this case they arrived with a show of force but after they made their point nobody saw them again]

March 9th 1892

Calvin Mcdowell, Thomas Moss, and Will Stewart are awaken by noise outside. A white militia had showed up to the jail house. 75 men with mask showed up and 9 of them entered the jail to grab the 3 men.

Masked Man 1: Well, look at what we have here. A few uppity niggers, who thought they could attack good Christian white men.

Masked Man 2: Do you know why I despise the nigger race boy?

Calvin Mcdowell: Sir, we just want to live in peace.

Masked Man 2: Hand me my shot gun. I'll shut this one up.

Calvin Mcdowell strikes Masked Man 2 and tries to wrestle the weapon away from him. Calvin grabs the mask and starts to pull it off the masked man as the two struggle.

Masked Man 2: This one is strong! Help me!

A third man shoots Calvin Mcdowell, blowing his fingers off with the shot gun. The other men begin to fight for their lives as Calvin is shot in the face. The third man stands over Calvin and shoots him in the face again. Thomas Moss was also shot and laid on the ground as two men aimed guns at him. The masked men had also called white reporters to witness the lynching.

Reporter: Can I tell your family anything sir?

Thomas Moss: Tell my people to head west. There is clearly no justice here!

(Masked Man 1 shoots Thomas Moss again in the head to stop him from talking.)

Masked Man 1: Why won't you die?

Thomas Moss finally passed away as Will Stewart continues to fight. He punches one of the men in the face and grabs the pistol off of his waste when he is shot twice. Will Stewart continues to fight, even as he bleeds but he is no match for the countless men.

Masked Man 1: You fancy nigger. Why couldn't you just accept your lot in life like the rest of your kind?

Will Stewart: I'm going to die a free man! I am a free man!

(Masked Man 1 one delivers the final shot that kills William Stewart.)

Masked Man 1: Let this be a lesson to all. Shelby County belongs to the white man. This is our county and this is our country. They should have gone back to Africa! There will be order or there will be nooses. Take your pick. These people will not mix in with our white kids!

[It has been highly suspected that William Barrett, the rival store owner was one of the masked men. He resented the successful business and wanted to put an end to their success. In reality, white supremacy was never about black people pulling themselves up by the bootstraps. The three men who were killed were polite, well-mannered and well-dressed people. They worked hard every day and had families. Entering a jail and removing the occupants was common practice at this point and the sheriff often was part of it or outnumbered.]

THE FINAL CHAPTER
IN THE 1877 SAGA

Ida gets dressed and fixes some food to take to her good friend Thomas Moss who is in jail. She steps out of her room where her aunt Fanny was waiting for her. Her Aunt Fanny slowly moves towards her and hugs her and starts to cry. Ida begins to cry too, she didn't want to say it but she knew Thomas was gone.

Ida B. Wells: I have to get this food to Thomas.

Fanny: I'm so sorry baby!

Ida B. Wells: No, I won't believe it. I don't believe you.

Fanny: Thomas was shot to death.

Ida B. Wells: Don't say that!

(John P. Buchanan, the governor of Tennessee gathers with his small cabinet. There is an uprising of coal miners due to them losing their wages due to a convict leasing system.)

John P. Buchanan: Delores, fetch me some tea darling. Get to the point Mr. Hill.

Mr. Hill: Sir, men down in Shelby County went into a jail and pulled out 3 Negro men awaiting trial. They shot them all to death.

John P. Buchanan: What do you suppose I do about it? Some niggers got killed. They should follow the law next time. Now they want to vote. I don't understand these people.

Mr. Hill: These men have constitutional rights now. The 14th Amendment is very clear about states and Federal government.

John P. Buchanan: As far as I am concerned, Lincoln over stepped his authority when he started his war of Northern aggression. I'm not following that constitution. See your way out.

Mr. Hill: It's the unconstitutional convict leasing that started the coal mining issue you're dealing with now. If they can grab Negro men off the street and force them to labor for free, why pay white men?

John P. Buchanan: Leave me alone. Close my door on your way out.

[Many Southern whites came up with a romantic version of slavery where slaves were well taken care of and "Yankees" started a war of Northern Aggression against the south. In reality, once Article 7 of the constitution was ratified, all states had agreed to join a union. People did not have a right to "unattach" a state from the union simply because they did not agree with slavery.]

Memphis Free Speech

In 1868 the 14th Amendment to the constitution was supposed to make black and white people equal under the eyes of the law. We were supposed to be protected as citizens. We pay taxes as citizens and our men should be allowed to vote as citizens. Thomas Moss was the best of us. Well spoken, well-educated and hard working. He was a well- liked man and dressed like a gentleman. William Barrett used the Sheriff's department and a judge in order to get rid of his economic competition. How can America be a great country when they are killing Negro men simply for being successful? Continue to boycott their trolley. Should they make money off of us? We built this country and now they are locking us out of our "just due". You can head west to Kansas as it was suggested before they killed Thomas. They clearly never planned on protecting our rights in the south. Respectable men, who pulled themselves up by the boot straps were shot down like dogs. They call us animals, but they treat animals much better than they treat us.

Iola

[African-American men had the right to vote on paper before all women. While earlier suffragettes were disgusted in the idea of black men having a right to vote, Ida B. Wells considered it a matter of life and death that they could vote. She wanted rights for herself but did not want those rights taken from black men because they got them first.]

A man waits outside of the office of Ida B. Wells. He

approaches her when she heads out to lunch.

Jim: Hey, why don't you stay in a woman's place?

Ida B. Wells: I am in a woman's place, at the top.

Jim: Where is your husband?

Ida B. Wells: Never mind you asking about my husband.

(The man gets angry and storms off.)

Ida B. Wells sets out to investigate a series of lynching but repeatedly is met with the justification of sexual assault. According to many white journalist, there was an epidemic of Negro men sexually assaulting white women. This didn't make sense to Ida because during the Civil War many southern white men left to fight in the war and their women remained untouched.

Adelia: The whites gathered around like a carnival and took pieces of his body after hanging him up in that tree.

Ida B. Wells: Cut him down. Is his…

Adelia: Yes, they cut his male part off and took it.

Ida B. Wells: What do you think they did with it?

Adelia: I don't know but it's supposed to be pay back for being a rapist.

Ida B. Wells: Can you get me the names of some of the women that were raped?

Adelia: How many do you need?

Ida B. Wells: All of them.

(Ida and Adelia head to the home of one of the victims. Betsy Mae steps outside to get her laundry.)

Betsy Mae: Can I help you? Aren't you in the wrong area?

Ida B. Wells: My name is Iola, I am with the press and I just wanted to first of all say I am sorry for what you have been through. As a woman…

Betsy Mae: I can't talk to you.

Ida B. Wells: Why?

Betsy Mae: Iola, is it? You're going to get me hurt. You might come up missing. Now get, go on now, get!

Ida B. Wells: Excuse me?

Adelia: No Iola, remember, we have another engagement. We have to go.

The two women (Ida and Betsy Mae) stare at each other in anger. Ida decides to walk away from Betsy Mae. A loud voice calls from the doorway of the house.

Bubba: Don't you bring your uppity nigger ass back here again!

Adelia: That was crazy! That man just called us the most disgusting word.

Ida B. Wells: That's normal in this line of work. Either that or they call you a wench. There is one more name on that list I want to check. I need to stop home first.

(Ida and Adelia make one more stop. A young lady is sitting outside on her porch when the two ladies approach.)

Ida B. Wells: My name is Iola and this is Adelia. I wanted to ask you some questions about your sister.

Mable: What about her?

Ida B. Wells: The Negro that raped her was just a boy?

Mable: Nobody raped that whore. She was a nigger lover. Sorry…

Adelia: Was?

Mable: She took her life after the men from the neighborhood killed that boy.

Ida B. Wells: Are you telling me she was not raped?

Mable: My sister loved that boy.

Ida B. Wells begin to investigate the claims of rape from the women. It turned out that the women had been having consensual sex with the men but when word got back to their family the men would be lynched. Some of the men were wearing white aprons and some had their male parts removed. Some of the men had families. Some of the white women were even married. All over the south black men were being killed for either having a successful business or sleeping with white women. In Arkansas, white residence literally were buying bus tickets and putting black men on the bus and making them leave. They were using the phrase "this town ain't big enough for the both of us".

Meanwhile the reputation and popularity of Ida B. Wells had grew. She was a very strategic planner and brilliant at executing her ideas. She had traveled to Kansas to take notes for residents who were now leaving Tennessee by the thousands thanks to her. Her voice was becoming powerful and everybody wanted a piece of "Iola".

Adelia: I know you want to write about what you discovered but we have to be careful.

Ida B. Wells: Did you know Thomas had a baby on the way?

Adelia: No.

Ida B.Wells: I can't be a coward. I won't be stupid but I can't sit silent. What happened to equal rights?

Adelia: I don't want you to end up in a tree with them.

(Ida B. Wells delivers her investigative findings in what will later be published in Southern Horrors)

Someone must show that the Afro-American race is sinned against more than they sin. I take no pleasure in exposing the lawlessness and corruption. What I am about to state will offend some but must be stated. Nobody in the South truly believes in an epidemic of Negro men raping white women. If Southern white men are not careful they will expose themselves as they have reached too far. The white masters were away for 4 years during the Civil War. You never heard of a white woman being touched or rape being a popular thing. It was not until the Negro was no longer his property and now can own property; that you hear of rampant rape. 8 men lynched since my last publication. The truth will serve as defense for the Afro-American Samson who finds themselves betrayed by white Delilah's.

The truth is the miscegenation laws of the south only limit Afro- American men and white women while leaving white men free to sleep with as many colored girls as he pleases. Ms. J.S. Underwood of Ohio confessed that she was dishonest about William Offett, the Afro-American man that she accused of rape while her husband, who was a minister, was away. The truth was published in the Cleveland Gazette, January, 16, 1892. She confessed that Offett use to bring chestnuts and candy for the kids while she would sit in his lap. She became afraid because the neighbors had seen her. William Offett served 4 years of his 15 year sentence after her husband found out the truth.

Sarah Clarke of Memphis was indicted for miscegenation, her defense was she was not white. There was a young country girl from Mississippi (Lilly Bailey) who received shelter at a woman's refuge until her Negro child was born. She would not reveal the name of the Negro who had "disgraced her". M. Strickland was jailed after being caught in a white woman's room. Mr. Strickland who was a furniture salesman was released after the white woman stated that she was "buying curtains" from him.

Frank Whims of Chattanooga only escape a lynching due to armed citizens protecting him until the jail cell was closed. He had handwritten letters of the white woman making an appointment with him. If the woman is of the superior race, does that not make her guiltier? Ebenezer Fowler, called the wealthiest colored man in Issaquena County, Mississippi, was shot down by a group of white men after passing letters back and forth with a white woman. Nobody in the South believes the "thread bare" lie that Negro men are raping white women.

When the actual victim of rape is a colored woman, it is different. There was the case of Pat Hanafin of Nashville Tennessee who raped a black girl and later become a detective in the city. There have also been cases where white militia have showed up to protect white men who have raped colored girls. Also an 8 year old girl named Maggie Reese was raped. The white man sat safely in his jail cell, the childhood of the colored girl did not matter.

In reality, the whites resent the new found freedom of the Negro. They often shout phrases like "this is a white man's country. You saw it with the violent overthrow of reconstruction. You saw it with the "Tilden or Blood campaign. Southern whites often view it as "intelligence against government and intelligence murdering ignorance". The record grows worse as the Afro-American grows in intelligence. It is time to thoroughly investigate lynch law.

William Barrett took a group of 12 deputized white men to The People's Grocery. The young men inside fired in self-defense but stop firing when they made it known they were law men. My good friend Thomas Moss was among the three lynched in a shocking manner to teach a lesson not to fire upon white men, not even in self-defense.

The whites in the South on one hand say "hands off" and to leave them to their own affairs while at the same time stealing the rights and taking everything from the males of the Afro-American race. He has been deprived of any redress and whites have adopted a total disregard for human life. Citizens are often allowed to go into jails, with no mask, where everybody knows them and simply demand the keys to the cell to kill young men.

The white man's God is the dollar and the Afro-American community make up about one – third of the South. Once we remove dollars it will begin to cripple them economically. You will gain nothing by attempting to appeal to the white man's conscience. There is no justice in the courts as white judges and juries skip over the rule of law and go along with their prejudices instead. The only case where lynching has not occurred is in Jacksonville, Florida and Paducah, Kentucky where the Negroes have taken up arms to prevent lynching. The white man should fear biting the dust every time he attacks the Negro as he is normally the aggressor. A Winchester rifle should find a place of honor in every Afro- American household.

The Gods help those who help themselves

Iola

[Ida B. Wells revealed that the white woman's word was strong enough to save her black lover or get him lynched. She often chose the ladder to save herself the embarrassment. She didn't look down on black males for sleeping with the white women because white men had been doing the same thing for centuries. She also made references to white Juliet betraying their black Romeo. She stated if the white race is so superior should they not be held to a higher standard when sleeping with Negroes, of course she stated it with sarcasm]

White newspapers and citizens grew angry.

Jim: That nigger is gone! She will die tonight!

Edward: How dare her insult white women, she must be found and brought to heel. Get the rope.

A group of white men showed up to destroy the office of Ida B. Wells. They also put a bounty on her head for her comments. They were out for blood and wanted her dead. To their surprise, she had already fled, heading up north to Chicago, avoiding the already crowded Kansas. The group of men burn down the printing press.

Europe

Ida B. Wells heads to London, Britain in order to get away from the United States. She looks around as she is taken back by how different everything was. She toured Europe and educated people on the plight of the American Negro. As the rest of the world had moved forward out of slavery itself, America held on to its peculiar system as long as it could. The white supremacy in Europe was a little more subtle but still present. At the same time Frances Willard of the Woman's Christian Temperance Union (WCTU) was traveling to talk about suffrage and the dangers of alcohol. The two women bump heads at a conference in front of reporters.

Frances Willard: The evil of alcohol, it brings out the sinful nature in men, it leads to a culture of criminals.

Ida B. Wells: What Ms. Willard is failing to mention is that most of these cases have nothing to do with rape at all. Whites in America are using lynching as a way to kill off black competition. The American Negro still is not free, even after the passing of the 14th amendment to the constitution.

Frances Willard: I am not saying alcohol only brings out the worst in colored men. I am saying alcohol brings out the worse in everyone. The WTCU has taken a stance against the barbaric practice of lynching.

Ida B. Wells: Ms. Willard uses the fear of Negro men to gather support for her cause. She is even friendly with segregationist. Any failure to pass legislation is usually passed off as blame because of the so called wicked Negro in the south. WCTU even allows segregation in its southern chapters. She has made disgusting comments like the "colored race multiplies like locust in Egypt".

Frances Willard leaves the press conference to head back to her hotel room. She had been quoted as saying terrible things about black people in the past. Ida B. Wells putting her on the spot was disturbing to her. She stares in anger at a distance as Ida B. Wells walks into her hotel.

[The suffrage movement had a worthy cause of voting rights for women but often would throw black men in particular under the bus to get their point across.]

1895

Ferdinand Lee Barnett: The Chicago Conservator is my baby. I already sold you part of it. I believe in you. Why don't you take control while I practice law?

Ida B. Wells: As long as I get to do it my way.

Ferdinand Lee Barnett: I would never stand in your way.

Ida B. Wells: I just have this vision.

Ferdinand Lee Barnett: I believe in you. What took you so long to walk into my life?

Ida B. Wells: Work and some men thought I was too smart for my own good.

Ferdinand Lee Barnett: What else are you working on?

Ida B. Wells: *A Red Record*

Ferdinand Lee Barnett: Sounds delightful.

Ida B. Wells: It's not supposed to…

(Sir, you have a phone call)

Ferdinand heads into his office and picks up the phone.

Rev. Collins: Frederick! Hey man!

Ferdinand Lee Barnett: minister, we haven't spoken in a long time. I was wondering about that speaking engagement.

Rev. Collins: That's why I gave you a ring. The leaders of the Southern Preachers Conference don't feel you would be a good fit, unless, you can calm your girl down.

Ferdinand Lee Barnett: We are about to get married

Rev. Collins: Yes, marry her but make sure she is the woman of the house. Make sure she stays in the woman's place.

Ferdinand Lee Barnett: Ida is free, she does what she wants.

Rev. Collins: Brother, I don't think you understand me.

Ferdinand Lee Barnett: Please don't call here again.

(Ferdinand Lee Barnett turns to see his future wife standing behind him.)

Ida B. Wells: Who was that?

Ferdinand Lee Barnett: Nobody, just some of the ministers are upset. They feel you're too outspoken.

Ida B. Wells: I speak because I have to speak. I am going to say what needs to be said and do what needs to be done for our people. If they were saying what needed to be said then I wouldn't have to say it…

Ferdinand Lee Barnett: You still miss Thomas…

Ida B. Wells: It's not just about Thomas anymore. It stopped being about him a long time ago.

Ferdinand Lee Barnett: Talk to me.

Ida B. Wells: We are supposed to be citizens, how can the government ignore our citizenship? Are we not a civilized nation? Why isn't anyone civil towards us?

Ferdinand Lee Barnett: Let's get married first and then it looks like you have some more work to do doesn't it?

(Ida nods her head)

Ferdinand Lee Barnett: Just one more thing…do you really need to keep that gun in here?

(Ida nods her head again)

Ida B. Wells: If I go then I'm taking one of them with me.

Ida B. Wells and Susan B. Anthony

Susan B. Anthony: Well, now you're Ms. Wells-Barnett.

Ida B. Wells-Barnett: I can hear a little bit of change in your tone when you mention my husband.

Susan B. Anthony: Women like us, we have a calling in life and it may cause you to lose focus.

Ida B. Wells-Barnett: Afro-American women have always had to work and take care of a family. The luxury of staying home is only afforded to white women.

Susan B. Anthony: Youth…

Ida B. Wells-Barnett: I still take issue at the fact that you only embraced Mr. Douglas when it didn't cost you southern white support. Now, you think I can't get the job done with a family. What is your problem with Afro-American men?

Susan B. Anthony: Frederick was a dear friend of mine.

Ida B. Wells-Barnett: But you would cut off your right arm before you support Negro men voting before you. Even when it's life or death that Afro- Americans get representation?

Susan B. Anthony: Til this day we still have not gotten the right to vote!

Ida B. Wells-Barnett: That's not the fault of Afro-American men. Even when they try to vote they get strung up in a tree. Those are our husbands, fathers, brothers and sons.

Susan B. Anthony: Men have always been placed over women!

Ida B. Wells: The smallest and most fragile white woman can have a Negro man killed with just her words. I don't think you get the power dynamic Ms. Anthony!

Susan B. Anthony: The Negro men who do vote. Do you think they would vote for women getting the right to vote? They're still men.

Ida B. Wells-Barnett: Perhaps you should tell your white men that they are men too.

Susan B. Anthony: There is more to be gained when we work together my dear? I am not the enemy.

Ida B. Wells: I will continue the fight until women have the vote. I will not be divided from our men. They didn't create this injustice. I don't want any limits placed on me for being a woman and I don't want any limits placed on men either. My husband is my support. He is more than willing to fight with me through the entire fight!

Susan B. Anthony: Well good for you Ms. Wells-Barnett. (sarcasm) If you're happy then I am happy for you.

Ida sipped her tea as her and Susan B. Anthony sat quietly. Susan B. Anthony had still not won the right to vote for women. She was older and you could tell that she was upset about the slow progress of the suffrage movement. Deep down, Ida still admired her for the times she had been arrested and had made bold statements and pushed for the equality of women in America. (scene)

The Machine

In Tuskegee, Alabama a man was pacing back and forth practicing a speech he was about to deliver in Atlanta.

Booker T. Washington: (Can we really view 1877 as the falling off point for the Negro? Did we move too fast to live among the white man? In a rush to appear the same as them. What benefit do Negro people have from learning Greek? Do you want to quote some dead white man from centuries ago, does that make you feel educated? Do you think that will earn you the respect of white people? In 1881 we established the Tuskegee Institute for a reason. I propose a compromise, we Negroes leave the whites alone and up to their own devices and we build. What good is knowing Greek when you have no home? If Negroes need houses then we will teach Negroes to build houses. You will learn skills and how to own your own business. In order to become a strong and powerful as white people, we have to build away from them.

The End of Act 1

ACT 2

Booker T. Washington: I say to you, cast down your buckets right here! Imagine what Atlanta can be. When we started the Tuskegee Institute in Alabama we didn't have buildings. We built them. You are never going to be one with white people. Learn to live with yourselves. It is the pushing and the pushing too fast that creates more tension. I met a Negro, who owned a piano but did not know how to play the piano. I don't find any dignity in being the poor version of white people. I find honor in being ourselves. Learn to tailor our own clothing, grow our own food and build our own buildings. There is no shame in maintaining the land. Every race has to start from somewhere and improve. When you can make your own water fountain why ask to drink from their water fountain young men and women?

(Crowd cheers as the donations flow into what is now known as Tuskegee University)

(Booker T. Washington had become a major contributor to the Black community and school had grown more and more powerful. Emmett Scott, the trusted advisor of Booker T. Washington enters the room)

Emmett Scott: Sorry to disturb you

Booker T. Washington: Wizard, how are you doing? How can I help you?

Emmett Scott: The Chicago Conservator put out a disturbing article concerning you and the Atlanta Compromise speech sir. Do you want me to make them go away?

Booker T. Washington: That's your department, I don't worry about press. Did you put George Washington Carver on staff like I told you?

Emmett Scott: Yes

Booker T. Washington: See to it that he enjoys his stay here.

(scene)

A newspaper decides to interview Ida B. Wells, now Ida B. Wells-Barnett. The Red Record had been published and she continued her investigations into the lynching going on in America.

Reporter: Ms. Barnett

Ida B. Wells-Barnett: My name is Wells- Barnett

Reporter: Yes, forgive me. You have caused a stir in the past by publishing that in your opinion, Negro men were being lynched for having successful businesses and sleeping with white women. You also stated that the sexual relations took place with consent and these women were not raped.

Ida B. Wells- Barnett: I stated facts. Some of the Negroes lynched were women. They don't have the male body part to rape these white women. Some of the women also admitted to being in pursuit of Negro men.

Reporter: Oh is that right!

(The reporter is now visibly upset)

Ida B. Wells- Barnett: That's right, these white women, many of them, have an affinity for Negro men.

Reporter: What's so special about Negro men that a white woman would want them?

Ida B. Wells- Barnett: You would have to ask them and while you're asking them you can also ask why the white men have been sleeping with and having babies with Negro women. Babies that they leave for Negro men to raise as their own.

Reporter: Why I'd never…

(The reporter mouth drops open)

Ida B. Wells- Barnett: Come on now, you know those white men use to sneak out to the slave quarters.

Reporter: You should be ashamed of yourself.

Ida B. Wells- Barnett: No, freedom of speech.

(Ferdinand Lee Barrett enters the office with lunch for Ida as the news reporter walks by him at a fast pace, very careful not to touch him. She was visibly angry.)

Ferdinand Lee Barnett: Another reporter

Ida B. Wells- Barnett: I may have ruffled a few feathers.

Ferdinand Lee Barnett: Well, most of my esteemed

colleagues enjoy your reporting, as do I. Did you really bite a train conductor?

Ida B. Wells-Barnett: Why does everyone keep asking me that?

Ferdinand Lee Barnett: I love you.

1903

The Jim Crow era was now fully underway and it has become common place to commit acts of random violence against black Americans. White people gathered all over the country to watch *Uncle Tom's Cabin* and make fun of black people as white actors put on black make-up or "black face" to put on an adaptation of an earlier released book.

W.E.B. Dubose: We have reached a point of being African and American. Two souls in one body in need of reconciliation. I published the Souls of Black Folks in order to assist with that reconciliation. During my studies at Harvard I was able to better myself by adding to my skills as a critical thinker. Booker T. Washington has decided to tell the Negro people to instead cast down their buckets at the bottom, where we belong, away from mainstream society. Booker T. Washington does not fully grasp the way society works. It will be a talented- tenth that brings the Negro population out of the dark and leads. I don't look down at the layperson who may lay bricks, I just understand that he will probably not lead us to where we need to be. The penalty for misleading can be costly.

1905

W.E.B. Dubose: Even in trying to meet up and discuss issues like other Americans we are being discriminated against. We have chosen to meet at Niagara Falls because we are starting The Niagara movement. The talented-tenth must speak truth to power in order to move the Negro forward in the country we built. I respect everyone who showed up here and put your reputations at stake for the movement.

William Monroe Trotter: I don't have any critique of the movement, I just think right now it will be safer and in our best interest to include men above all.

W.E.B. Dubose: Brother Trotter, are you saying you don't want women as a part of the movement?

William Monroe Trotter: I want us to go in the right direction.

W.E.B. Dubose: What will become of Ms. Wells-Barnett? Do you want her working with the likes of Booker T. Washington?

William Monroe Trotter: Can we finish the Declaration of Principles now?

W.E.B. Dubose: I want to "table" this other discussion for later. I don't know how you can be organized without women.

(scene)

Emmett Scott walks into a room full of black and white men to interrupt his boss Booker T. Washington. Booker T. Washington while not wanting to seem too uppity around whites still eagerly dismissed them knowing it must be important if Scott would barge into the room.

Emmett Scott: W.E.B. Dubose has gotten together with other Negroes to start a new movement. They're calling themselves the Niagara movement.

Booker T. Washington: What do I care about what they call themselves? Our machine is too big to stop.

Emmett Scott: But they are using your name, they are literally known for standing in opposition to you and your great work.

Booker T. Washington: Get rid of them.

Emmett Scott: How?

Booker T. Washington: Break their bank. Anyone who helps the Niagara movement will be an enemy of mine.

Emmett Scott: Ida B. Wells-Barnett is with them…

Booker T. Washington: I've come to like her husband. They have to go too. Nobody will give them assistance. They all ran from the south, they don't live here.

(Emmet Scott nods his head.)

(scene)

A young couple walks into a home in Louisiana. They are smiling and holding hands. A man is already in the living room planted on the couch with a rifle in his hand.

Jimbo: You were getting ready to rape my daughter

Becky: No daddy please

Jimbo: Shut up and sit down.

Young Bobby: No sir, we were just…

Jimbo: Go ahead and lie to me boy! I can kill you right now!

Young Bobby: Please sir, have mercy on me.

Jimbo: Did you have mercy on my daughter? You just came in and raped her. A good Christian girl and you have ruined her.

Becky: Daddy don't say that!

Jimbo: Shut your nigger loving mouth. Do you know what will happen if anyone finds out about this? You're running around with one of them!

Becky: But I love him!

Jimbo shoots the young man in the stomach. He falls to the ground. Young Bobby looks at the blood covering his hand and tries to crawl away.

Becky: If you kill him I'll tell everyone what I saw! You was sleeping with our maid!

Jimbo: You shut your mouth.

Becky: No, you're such a hypocrite!

Jimbo shoots Young Bobby again, this time in the head. Next he walks to the kitchen and grabs the maid Susy by the hair. He throws her on the ground right next to Young Bobby.

Susy: Please sir, I didn't see nothing.

Jimbo: See what you mad me do! Now I gotta kill her too.

Becky: No daddy please!

(Jimbo fires a shot, striking the maid in the head.)

Jimbo: This crazy animal, ran into our home. He shot Susy and he shot himself! You got that?

Becky looks at her father with tears flowing from her face. He gets closer to her and places the shotgun barrel on her chin. He places his finger on the trigger.

Becky: He came into our home and killed Susy.

Jimbo: Who came into our home and killed Susy?

Becky: Bobby did.

Jimbo: Say that animal did it!

Becky: No, he was a good boy.

Jimbo: Say it!

Jimbo grabs his daughter by the hair and drags her into her room and beats her. The Sheriff finally arrives with two of his men to take a look at the scene.

Sheriff Bigsby: He shot her and shot himself?

Jimbo: Yes sir, with this rifle.

Sheriff Bigsby: Isn't this your prize rifle, the one you hunt boars with?

Jimbo: Yes sir, he broke in and then took my rifle.

Sheriff Bigsby: Were you home?

Jimbo: No, I just came home. My baby girl saw everything. Becky! Becky!

(Becky walks out of her room with a bruised face and a busted lip.)

Sheriff Bigsby: What happened here sweety? What happened to your face?

Becky: My Daddy

(Sheriff Bigsby grabs her by the face and mushes her back until she is against the wall.)

Sheriff Bigsby: You stupid whore, the nigger did it! Say it! Say it!

(Becky is shocked that the Sheriff is in on it too. She looks at him with pain and hurt in her eyes.)

Jimbo: I tell you what…We are going to put your nigger loving ass in a "nut house"!

Becky: I didn't get raped.

The two men call one of their Doctor friends to come over and take a look at Becky. He does an examination at the home.

Doctor Bigsby: My brother was right. She is suffering from some type of hysteria. She has lost touch with reality.

Becky doesn't say anything. Sheriff Bigsby came from a powerful family. Her father Jimbo couldn't even save her now as he spits his tobacco out in the yard in anger. She has a sad look on her face as they restrain her to take her away. A small crowd gathers outside. They all watch while she is dragged away in to a medical facility.

Jimbo: There's nothing to see here. A nigger broke in and

killed my maid and hit my baby girl. Now she has gone mad!

(The white women in the crowd gasp and hold their chest as they imagine the horrible things Young Bobby had planned for the young lady.) (scene)

W.E.B. Dubose is making phone calls attempting to gain more support for the Niagara movement. Booker T. Washington has put a freeze on the money by taking a "either us or them stance". Meanwhile William Monroe Trotter is thinking of heading in a new direction and breaking off to start his own movement.

Mary Burnett Talbert: Any miracles happen yet?

W.E.B. Dubose: Booker T. has Carnegie and Rockefeller money. How does a Negro man build and sustain all of that power?

Mary Burnett Talbert: By promising to keep Negroes in the south and well hidden. White capital will flow in as long as they stay down south. The poor whites in the south don't mind us being close by as long as we are cleaning their homes. The wealthy whites in the north don't care if we have money as long as we stay away from them. Both sides don't want Negro men with their daughters. They're calling us radicals.

W.E.B. Dubose: They called Thaddeus Stevens a radical.

Mary Burnett Talbert: Right now, you might as well call Washington the most powerful Negro in America. They have a Negro down there who can do 100 things with a peanut. A peanut.

W.E.B. Dubose: William may be leaving the movement soon.

Mary Burnett Talbert: You may lose some people but you can gain some people.

W.E.B. Dubose: Where is Ms. Wells-Barnett in all of this? (scene)

Adelia arrived in Louisiana, she received a letter from one of the friends of Becky. She had been placed in a mental facility after the killing of Young Bobby. His parents were beside themselves. Before heading to the facility to see Becky, Adelia stopped to speak with the parents of Young Bobby.

Bobby Senior: Everybody know Bobby was running around with that white girl. I met her before myself. I called myself trying to warn him.

Adelia: He kept seeing her after you warned him?

Bobby Senior: I figured boys will be boys.

Adelia: In the south?

Bobby Senior: Do you have a son Ms.

Adelia No.

Bobby Senior: I thought Ms. Wells-Barnett was coming to see me.

Adelia: She is not welcome in the south. Do you know the name of the hospital Becky is in?

Bobby Senior: Yes.

(Adelia is dropped off at the hospital, she heads in to see Becky. She is sitting at a table with restraints on her. Her hair was frizzy and she looked un-kept but she was alert.)

Becky: Are you here for the story?

Adelia: I want to help you, I need to know what they are covering up first.

Becky: Young Bobby didn't attack nobody. They tried to say he raped me.

Adelia: Who shot Young Bobby and Susy?

Becky stops talking…

Adelia: Ain't you gonna tell me? I want to help you here.

Becky: (laughs) you can't help me. You can't help yourself. You seem like a nice lady but you don't know where you're standing.

Adelia: Where?

Becky: The White League owns the south. Down here they are God.

Adelia looks up to see Sheriff Bigsby coming towards her at full speed. She runs out of the door as one of the deputies try to catch up with her. Luckily her ride had been waiting for her outside. Adelia heads back to Chicago to tell Ida the news. A cover up with the Sheriff involved. After a long journey Adelia meets at a hotel near Buffalo. She is directed to a door as a man stands guard with a rifle. He steps aside for Adelia and knocks on the door three times. His heavy hand slaps the door. (bang bang bang). Ida B. Wells-Barnett opens the door. She is sitting with

W.E.B. Dubose and Mary Burnett Talbert. She walks in and the door slams shut. (scene)

August 1908

Springfield, Illinois

Mabel Hallam is having sex with her white lover when she heard her husband headed towards the home. The man gets away and makes off behind the home into the surrounding area. Mabel runs outside and starts screaming.

Mabel Hallam: Help! A nigger just raped me! Help!

Her husband rushed to her aid. He called the Sheriff's department and they went searching for the imaginary black man who Mabel claimed raped her. A nearby carrier working in the area, George Richardson, was picked up and arrested for the rape of Mabel Hallam. Sheriff Werner places George Richardson in a cell next to a man named Joe James. The white mobs begin making phone calls to Sheriff Werner attempting to gain access so that they could lynch the two men.

White rioter 1: Sheriff Werner, you can't hide those niggers in there for long. Come out now and we will just have a little talk with them.

Sheriff Werner: Now, you stop calling here right now!

Deputy: What are we going to do boss?

Sheriff Werner: Get me a car, I am going to get these men out of town.

Joe James: Thank you sir.

Sheriff Werner: Don't thank me yet. You are still going to be punished for your crime, just not by a mob.

(Sheriff Werner sneaks the two men out in a car that he barrowed. The mob learns that the men are gone and work themselves into a frenzy.)

White Rioter 1: Curse Lincoln for freeing those niggers! Kill them all!

White Rioter 2: Protect our white women at all cost.

Newspapers start calling for reinforcements as more people arrived in Springfield. They broke into a local pawn shop and started stealing the guns. The white league arrives to help

Thurman: Yeah! The White League has arrived to help you with your little problem.

The White League members start to load up their weapons. They pass guns out to men who don't have any. The angry mob heads down to "The Levee" (where the black owned businesses were). They start to break into the black owned businesses and beat on the owners while stealing their property. The rioters sat outside drinking stolen beer and cursing President Lincoln for freeing the slaves. A man named Scott Burton travelled from his home to protect his barbershop. The angry mob shot Scott Burton to death and then strung him up in a tree while firing shots through his already lifeless body. A man walks outside of his business to see what the commotion is but runs back in as the mob spot him and run towards the business. The actual owner, who was a white man steps out.

Shop keeper: Hey, this here is a white business. You son of a bitches don't touch my property.

White Rioter 1: We are sorry sir. Do you mind sending that nigger out so that we can have a talk with him?

Shop keeper: He works for me.

White rioter 2: Are you saying you're going to protect that criminal?

The shop keeper throws his black employee out of the shop and the white mob beats him to death and then ties him to a car and drags his lifeless body down the street. The angry mob destroy most of the black and Jewish owned businesses. One of the men stops and slaps a little infant baby out of the hands of his mother and walks away as the woman screams.

White rioter 1: Where do all the niggers live?

Thurman: They call it The "Badlands".

White rioter 1: Well let's go see how bad those niggers are! Yeah!

The angry white mob shoots bullets in the air as they head towards The Badlands to kill the black residents next. The residents already heard the white mob is on the way. Many grab what they can and head out of Springfield as they are met with threats from outside counties to keep moving, and to not stop for rest. A young man sits in one of the abandoned homes named Shooter. He is loading up his rifle and waiting for the mob to arrive. His mother and father have already left town but shooter stayed. Shooter grabs an extra box of ammo and then says a quick prayer before heading out of the door.

Hundreds of members of the white mob head into the

Badlands. Shooter lays on one of the roof tops waiting. Shooter takes aim and shoots one of the rioters in the head. He hits the ground as others take cover and start shooting at the homes. Shooter kisses his father's Civil War hat and then takes aim and kills another rioter. A bunch of men break off and start to head in Shooter's direction. As Shooter attempts to make another kill the rioters pin him down by shooting 20 bullets his way. Shooter kisses the hat again while the mob makes their way to him. Another rioter is shot but this time it wasn't by Shooter. The state militia had been called and they arrived with rifles. They shot a few of the rioters after their warning shots were ignored. Shooter finds time to make his escape as the militia fires at the rioters.

The next day more and more militia arrived to try to stop the mob which is now in the thousands. Men are outside selling items from the black people that they killed. Many of the black families fled or were hiding in the State Armory until the mob left. The mob attempted to get into the armory to kill the black residents but the militia would not allow them in. Shooter slips by in the commotion after he tosses his gun in the bushes and acts like a lost little boy so that the armory will allow him in for shelter. The angry mob can't find anymore residents to kill so they started drinking, partying, and looking for things to loot.

Thurman: Hey, you must have a small colored population here. Where did they all run off to?

White rioter 2: We could go to the Donnigan house. There one of those mix breeding couples. Taking our jobs and our women!

Thurman: The White League only kills other whites in self- defense. We don't kill our own.

White Rioter 2: Let's just kill Donnigan.

Mr. Donnigan can hear the commotion outside. He had decided to stay home and protect his wife during the rioting and looting by the white mob. He peeked in the room to make sure she was ok and then went to check on the commotion. One of the rioters had already broken through the door and was standing in the Donnigan's kitchen. Mr. Donnigan looks on as several other men walk through the door with a rope and several guns.

(scene)

1909

Henry Moskowitz: I think we can all agree on the human rights aspect of the organization.

Mary Church Terrell: Equal rights for all people, complete equality. We should not have to live under two Tennessee's or two America's in fact.

Mary Burnett Talbert: Women have to also have a role in the organization. We will not sit quiet or in the back as support.

W.E.B Dubose: Yes, of course. I would not have it any other way.

Mary Church Terrell: You're mighty quiet over there Ms. Wells-Barnett. What are thinking about?

Ida B. Wells-Barnett: I was thinking about Booker T. Washington. What are they leaving out? They often cover the basics. If you can teach a Negro to bake bread then they can feed themselves. I don't disagree with that point. Then you get to the next floor in his intellectual building and we understand that if a Negro wants a home, they should learn to lay bricks. Then you reach the highest floor in his intellectual building and it is business. If you teach a Negro how to provide services then he has a business.

W.E.B. Dubose: I am aware of Booker T. Washington's philosophy.

Ida. B. Wells- Barnett: There should be more to his building. People who think like Mr. Washington miss a very important point. What holds all of this stuff in place?

What holds society in place? Laws, citizenship, if we don't have real citizenship then everything easily gets washed away. Somewhere hidden under all of that ego, he has to agree. Our political message and our politics must be geared towards citizenship. The lynching is lawless, they are breaking law.

Mary White Ovington: We can't just focus on the south. Last year the race riots of Illinois left 16 people dead. Thousands of whites attempted to take mob action against Negroes. When they were sent away to safety, the city was nearly destroyed. They rioted and looted and burned black businesses to the ground. Almost 100 Negro men and women lost their homes or business and any white person thought to be a lover of colored people were also attacked. The state militia had to come in and fight back. The riots in Springfield must be the last. They literally ran Negro people out of town. A town they helped build. I have seen Booker T. Washington speak before and he is brilliant but to compromise with people who riot and loot and destroy Negro people's homes just don't seem right.

W.E.B. Dubose: I propose that the Niagara Movement which has been dissolved and The National Negro Committee put everything we have into the world's most powerful movement. We will call it the NAACP. The National Association for the Advancement of Colored People.

Ida B. Wells- Barnett: Thank you Mary and Mary and the other Mary. You can never have enough Mary's. Thank you to all of the Founding members as we prepare to change the lives of everyone in America.

(scene)

Booker T. Washington stands before the National Negro Business League speaking about their continued growth. He was successful in slowing the spread of the Niagara Movement but his opposition had returned as the NAACP. They now had more resources and white members with connections, making it harder for "The machine" to destroy their influence.

Booker T. Washington: While they continue to protest and protest and protest, we continue to build institutions. We continue to build wealth and knowledge, even in the heart of the south. We are not going to base our lives on what white people think or even on what white people do. We do not wish to gain access to their citadels of power but instead let the Negro have his own. Prior to emancipation my family never had the opportunity to even sit down and have a quiet meal but instead children were fed scraps like animals. Now we grow our own food for us. It is easy for Mr. Dubose to critique from his perceived high place. We don't need a seat at their table but rather our own table.

(Members give a standing ovation)

Booker T. Washington walks off the stage and heads to the back where he meets "The Wizard", Emmett Scott.

Booker T. Washington: Did you send the donations off?

Emmett Scott: Yes, but boss I have to ask… Why not become allies with the NAACP since you secretly send donations to radicals anyway? People hate that you don't embrace them.

Booker T. Washington: They are grasping with both hands. We have the patience of a monument. We are growing powerful right under white people's nose. They'll never see us coming. Mr. Dubose and Ms. Wells- Barnett literally undermine me. They don't have the vision. I have the power to make a white man vanish if I wanted to. People who have never touched real power cannot understand it.

(scene)

Adelia returns to Louisiana with a white attorney from the NAACP. They head back to the hospital. Sheriff Bigsby is not there to meet them this time. Adelia eased in with a sigh of relief. The attorney stands back while Adelia speaks with one of the nurses. She breaks down crying after being told that Becky had hung herself and taken her own life. The attorney is there to comfort her as she cries. Even white girls like Becky have been destroyed and swept under the rug as collateral damage. Nobody had stopped to think that they also had a right to date or marry whoever they wanted to. The white supremacist held a deep belief that it is some form of genocide if a white woman decided to bring children into the world that were not white. With new Immigrants arriving from Europe it was becoming increasingly more difficult to know what "white" was. The new Immigrants also quickly embraced whiteness and learned to harbor anti-black racism while enjoying the fruit from the country built by black people.

(Scene)

1913

March 3

Alice Paul: Why are Negro women coming to the march?

Assistant: They have become highly influential and many of them are members of the NAACP who are pro women's rights.

Alice Paul: Make sure they march in back, out of sight. I will not bow down to the colored people like Susan B. Anthony tried to do! The National Woman's Suffrage Association belongs to us. We will not allow them to dictate.

Assistant: Yes maam.

[Thousands of women marched on Washington as Woodrow Wilson prepared to take office. The Suffrage movement had kicked into full swing thanks to Alice Paul and her new and fresh ideas. Her goal was to focus on a 19th Amendment to the constitution. Woodrow Wilson had other things in mind coming into office like introducing a Federal income tax and a Federal Reserve banking system. The women were met by angry mobs of men who were throwing things and hitting women. The police also refused to protect the women who decided to march on Washington. White men were injuring white women for attempting to vote and other white men refused to protect them. The site was confusing to Ida B. Wells because white men made it seem as if the protection of white women were the top priority when they wanted to lynch black men but not when they wanted to vote.]

Mary Church Terrell showed up with the mighty Delta Sigma Theta Sorority from Howard University. She was also one of the founders of the Colored Women's League or CWL. She was also a founding member of the NAACP along with Ida B. Wells. Ida had grabbed the Chicago member's delegation flag and headed to the front of the march where the black women were forbidden to go. Alice Paul looks over and see's Ida B. Wells, the frown on her face grew and grew as Ida B. Wells-Barnett smirked.

Marcher: Hey! Colored women are supposed to go to the back of the march!

Ida B. Wells-Barnett: No, I don't take orders from you or Alice Paul.

Marcher: You coloreds never know your place do you?

Ida B. Wells-Barnett: I do know my place, at the top!

Some of the marchers frown but a few embrace Ida as she proudly marches at the front of the Chicago delegation. After all, she helped build it.

Angry white mob member: Hey! They have a nigger marching up front!

(Ida B. Wells- Barnett waves at him as he almost explodes from his anger.)

Ida B. Wells- Barnett: Hi!

Angry white mob member: Oh, you uppity nigger…

Alice Paul's Assistant: Would you like me to remove her from the front?

Alice Paul: Are you insane? Do you know who that is? (scene)

[By Summer of 1914 an assassination of Arch Duke Ferdinand and already raised tensions, led to Germany going to war over Austria-Hungary against France who had an alliance with Russia and Britain. Germans attempt to go through neutral Belgium making matters worse. Both sides begin to expand into what they call a new frontier resulting in death on the continent of Africa. The Ottoman Empire decides to enter the World War and after a few initial loses uses the opportunity to commit mass genocide against Armenians.]

1915

November

Booker T. Washington was still traveling and was still the principal of the Tuskegee Institute. He had built a massive network that could not be matched. Emmett Scott was still his right hand and ran the school while he was away. Booker T. Washington collapses while talking to a small group of business leaders. He is rushed to the Doctors office. Booker T. didn't have long to live and shortly after died from complications from hypertension. They had got him back to Tuskegee University to see what he had built one more time before he died. Emmett Scott, who was assumed to be the "heir apparent" was passed over to replace Washington as principle.

By the time Booker T. Washington died he was the most powerful black man in America. He stayed in the south until he died. He had secretly used Tuskegee University to hide black people from local white lynch mobs in the area. He even helped some of them get out of town. He wrote an autobiography titled *Up from Slavery* and became one of the most powerful speakers in U.S. History. Marcus Garvey arrived in the United States in search of Booker T. Washington who had already died. Marcus Garvey was inspired by his black owned institutions.

[While the comic franchise X-Men was based on a battle of ideas between Malcom X and Dr. Martin Luther King Jr. the actual school for the gifted seems to be rooted in Booker T. Washington's University When Booker T. Washington passes away it leaves a power vacuum of people wanting to be the next top Negro.]

The End of Act 2

ACT 3

Ida B. Wells-Barnett, now 53 was still active but had removed herself from the main stage to work on taking care of her family. America had been shipping goods overseas to support France and Britain. Germany raged on but had grown weaker due to a lack of resources. Germany kept sinking American ships and ships with American passengers, eventually dragging the United States into the Great War. The same black men who had been denied their rights were asked to go fight for America in a foreign land. The U.S. was segregated and many black soldiers fell under the command of the French who treated them like humans, which confused the men because they were used to being treated like animals in America.

Shooter, who was one of the young men attacked in Springfield, Illinois joined the Harlem "Hellfighters". The 369th infantry fought side by side with the French. The Germans gave them the nick name of the "Hellfighters". Most black men were forced to be support and were not allowed to fight in combat. Many of the 369th infantry were awarded with the highest honors of the French army.

East St. Louis, Illinois 1917

Gerald: I have an idea that could possibly stop the labor strikes.

Callister: I'm listening…

Gerald: Can you bring me more colored people from Mississippi to work?

Callister: They mostly just stop through on their way to Chicago, but I can probably get one of my porter friends to spread the word that we have jobs. We can pay them half of what we pay the whites. Why do you want to offer them jobs?

Gerald: There is a war going on, no more Immigrants from Europe. I prefer the Immigrants.

(The tension was so great that the National Guard was called in, they had helped keep a lid on the violence. Angry white mobs begin to gather and plan and plot on how to put a stop to Negro labors coming up from the south to replace white workers who were going on strike. The all white unions did not allow black members effectively making themselves weaker and open to being replaced).

[Post Bacon's Rebellion changed the relationship between whites and blacks dealing with labor. While America had started off as a penal colony with Australia they eventually created a new system which raised whites above peasant status and plummeted black people to animal status. White supremacist often use the excuse of "blacks enslaving other blacks" as justification for mistreating black people but white people were placed in shackles by other white people. Both groups arrived the same way]

Bubba Hicks: The white League has arrived. How many niggers are we killing?

Brody: Hey brother, you can join in on the fun. I don't think you heard, we got a special treat.

Bubba Hicks: What kind of special treat?

(Brody opens his car door and shows his white hood)

Brody: The Klan has returned brother. The legendary Knights of the Ku Klux Klan.

[The white supremacist often used Knights as a symbol for racist groups because it goes back to a historical connection between The Knights Templars and Moors who left African and Arabia heading into southern Europe]

Bubba Hicks: You won't need no sheet. The Police Chief already gave us the ok. They won't shoot any white people.

Brody: Let's drive around and see if we can spot some niggers.

The two men drive around in a black car. They take turns shooting at random black people as they drive by. They drive by a group of men standing outside and shoot as the crowd breaks up and the men run, hiding behind whatever they could find. The two men laugh and drive off. Another car drives by and creeps up on the men. One of the men who had their own gun shot as the car takes off fast.

[Later we learn that the men in the second car are cops. Detectives in a similar Ford model T. unmarked police car.

Word gets back to the white mob that one of the detectives died. In this story Brody and Hicks are the men in the original Model T. but we are not sure if the police did the shooting and came back for more]

Brody: They killed a law enforcement officer. Let's move, come on time to get started.

Bubba Hicks: Thank you Jesus!

The men drive up to the train station and see two black men waiting on a ride. They had just got off of the train. The angry mob runs up to the men and starts to beat them with bats. One of the men crawl away begging for help as the mob beats on him. They string him up in a nearby tree and then begin to riddle his body with bullet holes. The mob continues on killing any black person within site.

Bubba Hicks: Hey Brody, the women want to know if they can join in.

Brody: Yee haw!

The mob heads over to a fountain park where a group of African-Americans are looking at the water. The mob pushes one person into the fountain and then they begin to beat on people. They tie one man to a car and drag his body as they race down the street. Police stop and give orders for the rioters to stop but were also given orders not to touch a single white person, after a while they move on allowing the black men and women to be killed.

The white mob lays a bunch of boards on the ground beat, then they almost beat a man to death. Afterwards they set him on fire and begin to cook his body on the wood. The women dance around the fire with joy and glee as they burn the man to death. You can hear the screams. The men and women of East. Louis head over the bridge into St. Louis, Missouri to get away from the mob violence as they begin to burn down the homes of the black residences. The rioters run up to a man who owns a car and pulls him out of the car and starts to beat on the man.

In the middle of the killing, the rioters begin to take photos and even cut the body parts off of some of them men. They leave a trail of dead bodies hanging from trees with their male parts missing. The symbol from black manhood that made whites feel uneasy. As the mob violence clears up almost a few hundred dead bodies lay in the streets as the white mob celebrates the return of the Ku Klux Klan.

Brody: Weeee! You better not come back here no more niggers! Stealing jobs from the white man!

As the mob passes by the fountain park again on the way out, one of the bodies is still moving. Brody shoots them one last time to make sure they are dead.

(Scene)

(W.E.B. Dubose enters a room. Ida B. Wells-Barnett is sitting at a desk working on a response to the violence in East St. Louis. She pretends not to see him.)

[Ida B. Wells Barnett left the NAACP a few years after helping found it. She was critical of the white leadership and many had thought Ms. Well-Barnett was too extreme. She believed in self-defense, even against crooked law enforcement as she had written on Mob Rule in New Orleans]

W.E.B. Dubose: Are you going to just pretend like I am not here?

Ida B. Wells-Barnett: How can I help you?

W.E.B. Dubose: The NAACP will be doing a silent march in response to the violence in East St. Louis. We could sure use your support. I know you left but…

Ida B. Wells-Barnett: Do you expect to get something done with your white leadership?

W.E.B. Dubose: We are benefitting from their resources and support. The Tuskegee machine was too powerful.

Ida. B. Wells-Barnett: Mr. Washington is dead. The "battle" is over. Nobody won. Negros lost.

W.E.B. Dubose: We can agree to disagree

Ida B. Wells-Barnett: You removed my name as a founder to the NAACP. It's like I didn't even help found it.

W.E.B. Dubose: It is like you didn't even help found it.

Ida B. Wells-Barnett: Well congratulations William.

W.E.B. Dubose: There is a new kid, he is gaining followers fast and he is too extreme. He's even more extreme than you.

Ida B. Wells-Barnett: Mr. Garvey, so I've heard. Listen, I am busy. I must respond to the violence in East St. Louis and I have a family to take care of.

(scene)

The Chicago Defender

America drafted Afro-American men to go off and fight their wars in the name of democracy. Yet when these soldiers return they are returning to a country where they are not protected by democracy. This is hypocrisy under President Woodrow Wilson! At what point do we get pass the talking and marching. If the 14th Amendment will not protect us then perhaps the 2nd Amendment will. Lynch law is barbaric savagery, how dare these people talk about how violent Negro men are when they have done nothing except commit violence against Negro Men, women, and children.

If our country, that we built will refuse to protect us, then we have a God given right to protect ourselves. We can't rely on black organizations that have been co-opted by white people, they are controlled opposition at this point. The fear of Afro-American men just being men is devastating to the American social order, why? Is black male masculinity so powerful that you fear it? They are now attacking women and children, well over 100 Afro-American women lynched now as well. When a group of people start attacking your children that's when you should be ready to die! 14th Amendment or 2nd Amendment!

Iola

Ida B. Wells-Barnett steps out of her house but is met by two agents. A young 22 year old by the name of Edgar J. Hoover was coming to power. His biggest target was Marcus Garvey but Ms. Well-Barnett had landed on a watch list.

Agent Smith: Good morning Ms.Wells-Barnett.

Ida B. Wells-Barnett: How can I help you officer

Agent Smith: Oh, you guessed I was an officer

Ida B. Wells-Barnett: Can I help you?

Agent Smith: What did you mean in your recent article, 14th Amendment or 2nd Amendment?

Ida B. Wells-Barnett: Have you read the 14th and the 2nd Amendment? You look federal to me. Don't you have access to federal laws?

Agent Smith: Yes, I have read the entire constitution

Ida B. Wells-Barnett: Then you should know what the 14th and the 2nd Amendment states. I am following your law.

Agent Smith: I won't take up any more time

Ida B. Wells-Barnett: Hey, have you guys done anything to investigate the people who are setting off bombs in Chicago?

Agent Smith: There's a war coming. Choose carefully Ms. Wells-Barnett. Have a good day now. (scene)

Marcus Garvey had arrived in America and become powerful very quickly. Some of the black leaders took him for a joke. He was young but a hard working. He opened a branch in New York of the Universal Negro Improvement Association. His goal was to unite Afro-Carribean's with African –Americans.

Marcus Garvey: The lynching in E. St. Louis was totally disrespectful and an evil act. Every African should be prepared to pick up weapons and defend ourselves against this evil. If they lynch us here, then it is only right we lynch them in Africa. Africa is going to be for Africans once again. Under the red, black, and green flag we will rise. The Bible says that we are made in the image of God. We can never be under a white man. Mr. Dubose and the NAACP are calling for peaceful chats. Peaceful chats in response to murder? Peaceful chats in response to lynching? I will be beginning a 38 city tour to bring unity to Africans in America. Because we have no unity they have taken advantage and if they fire upon us then we fire back!

[Agents watched from the crowd as Marcus Garvey activated the crowd. The U.S. government now viewed him as a real threat.]

1919

A vendor by the name of George Tyler walks into the offices of Marcus Garvey and shoots him several times and then walks out. Marcus Garvey survives the assassination attempt. His reputation begins to grow more and become that of a legend who survived gunshots. People begin to believe he was sent by God.

A young man by the name of Eugene Williams is swimming to shore at Lake Michigan when he is spotted by a group of white people who begin to stone him. They start throwing big and heavy stones, trying to injure the young man. The young boy drowns to death. As black people begin to protest all over white mobs begin to form in cities all over America to start attacking black people. They were also upset, at the "uppity" image of the black men that had return from World War 1 expecting to be treated like citizens.

(A young man arrives in Chicago and grabs his rifle from his car.)

Shooter: Hey guys! You might want to get in the house. I heard a lynch mob is headed for Chicago.

Bria: We know, we have decided to use the 2nd Amendment in Chicago. You're standing in "Ida B. Wells country".

Shooter: Well, I was attacked in Springfield when I was a boy. I just came back from the Great War.

Eddie: Well, welcome to the end of the world buddy. (scene)

(Ferdinand L. Barnett gathers with Ida, they send their children off to safety and load up their guns.)

Ferdinand L. Barnett: How are you feeling?

Ida B. Wells-Burnett: One had better die fighting against injustice then to die like a dog or a rat in a trap.

Ferdinand L. Barnett: If anybody comes through that door, I want you to hit them with every bullet you have, do you hear me?

Ida B. Wells-Barnett: I will… every single bullet

While Ida and her husband were able to stay off the radar

of the mob, the white mob did start attacking the Negro population. They begin to break into stores on the South Side of Chicago. A young boy wonders out into the street as the white mob raged on, looting and shooting. The young boy's mother tries to run and grab his hand when she is spotted. One of the white men shout nigger and then takes aim at the woman. Someone fires a single shot hitting the white man, he goes down.

Shooter: Get your son and go hide! Now!

Shooter and a group of black men and woman begin to mount a defense to run off the white looters. Shooter quickly moves his rifle from person to person, knocking down white looters like bowling pins. Bria and Eddie start shooting as well. The white mob turns and runs as they are met with a hail of gun fire. Bria shakes shooters hand. He reloads and waits for more looters to return. Bria was a young lady who grew up on the South Side of Chicago. She grew up reading work by Ida B. Wells-Barnett. Ms. Barnett had raised a generation of young women prepared to fight back.

Elaine, Arkansas

A small team of journalist make their way to Arkansas. They head to Helena to talk to a group of men who had been imprisoned after the deadliest of the riots. The woman is dressed like an elderly lady, she walks in with assistance from her team. She looks up at one of the men, to his surprise it was Ida B. Wells-Barnett. She had returned to the south, even with the bounty on her head.

[Ida B. Wells wore a disguise to sneak back into the south due to a bounty on her head]

Frank Hicks: It wasn't no black insurrection, they simply didn't want us to have a union. We started trying to get real pay. You could produce all day for a farm an end up owing money to the land owner. How can a worker end up owing money? We placed armed security outside because of all the riots and looting that was going on all over the country. I guess they got offended and started shooting. Our security shot back and the next thing you know they were rounding up Negros.

Ida B. Wells-Barnett: You confessed?

Frank Hicks: They tortured us all night. They shocked us, beat us, kept us up all night with no sleep. We had to confess to get a piece of bread and water.

Ida B. Wells-Barnett: All because you formed a union?

Frank Hicks: We were planning to sue them.

Ida B. Wells- Barnett: What did you witness once the fighting started?

Frank Hicks: Well, they rounded up every Negro they could find. You could either go with them or die. The police was on the side of the whites.

(Frank Hicks is taken back to his cell and Frank Moore was able to speak next)

Frank Moore: Army troops showed up, we ran out of hiding for help and they starting shooting too.

Ida listened as the men one by one provided her with facts

and locations to send her investigators. Men, women, and children were shot down. Law enforcement and the military joined in on killing black people. Fighting broke out in over 10 different areas. People ran towards the swamps to avoid the machine guns. They rounded up black people in mini concentration camps. All laws had been suspended. When they were finished well over 100 black people were killed.

(Ida packed up her notes and got ready to leave when one of the men called out to her.)

Ed Hicks: Excuse me, maa'm.. The Ku Klux Klan is back and this time they are the police.

Ida B. Wells-Barnett: What did you just say?

Ed Hicks: The Klan, they are the police now.

(scene)

Moore V. Dempsey

United States Supreme Court 1923

The Supreme Court Justices meet in chambers.

James C. McReynolds: Let's all just take a deep breath and slow down. Understand what you are doing. If you go back out there and side with the Negro, you will destroy a long standing precedent.

Oliver W. Holmes Jr.: Precedent? You mean backroom deals.

James C. McReynolds: Come on guys, you want the

constitution to protect Negros? Any nigger who screams their rights were violated will come knocking at the door of our court.

(Chief Justice Taft stands up)

George Sutherland: What he meant was we don't understand the gravity of the situation.

Oliver W. Holmes Jr.: It is settled, we will follow The Constitution of the United States, not some backroom deal to make Negroes second class citizens. The 14th Amendment, due process, it all matters. I will not disrespect The Constitution. We can't allow mob rule in America. They were really bold to stand in the courts making threats.

George Sutherland: We will be forgotten about in history! Don't do this.

Oliver W. Holmes Jr.: The majority agrees with me. You are welcome to dissent on the record. This ruling does not grant them their freedom but the case needs careful examination and if the case was determined by mob rule then it is void. You can't pretend to have a trial when it is already decided that someone will be found guilty no matter what. (scene)

[Ida B. Wells returned home after losing the run for President of the National Association for Colored Women. She was defeated by Mary Bethune who later founded Bethune-Cookman University. She was there when the organization was founded but once again people had decided to move away from her]

Ferndinand L. Barnett: They said you were too radical and not diplomatic enough?

Ida B. Wells- Barnett: I guess everyone is tired of me. Perhaps I stepped on too many powerful toes. I said what needed to be said. I would do it all again if I had to.

Ferndinand L. Barnett: Mary Bethune huh?

Ida B. Wells-Barnett: She is fairly young but smart. I still don't believe in limitations on women. I'm glad I could pave the way for her.

Ferndinand L. Barnett: You seem so sad dear. The children and I will never forget what you did. You saved the lives of thousands of people and put your life at risk, even with children to take care of. No organization can make you or break you. Not the NAACP and nobody else. I will never let you go.

Ida B. Wells-Barnett hugs on her family as they all gather in the living room to cheer her up. Ida B. Wells-Barnett Jr. gives her a big hug. They all talk throughout the night, lifting the spirits of Ms. Wells-Barnett. March 25th, of 1931 at the age of 68, Ida B. Wells-Barnett dies of uremia. She didn't get to finish her autobiography *A Crusade for Justice*.

[Later a young man by the name of El- Hajj Malik El-Shabazz would speak out against the NAACP]

Malcom X: We are not going to allow ourselves to be sidetracked fighting the NAACP or CORE, or the Urban League. Every President that has been elected by the NAACP in 51 years has been white. There should be some

Negro in there who is qualified to be president. Every time you have an integrated organization a white man always end up on top of it. I'm suspicious…it's just not intelligent for a black body to have a white head.

Til this day, the NAACP still has Ida B.Wells-Barnett removed from the Civil Rights Leader section but they have anti-lynching bill listed as one of their mile stone accomplishments. Lynching is still not a Federal Crime in the United States of America. Ida B. Wells-Barnett has her name on many schools and buildings throughout the United States, but her name has been largely overshadowed by others like Malcom X. Part of the ideology for common sense and self-defense adopted by Malcom X originated with Ida B. Wells-Barnett.

Ida B. Wells-Barnett was laid to rest at Oak Woods Cemetery in Chicago Illinois at the age of 68.

W.E.B. Dubose eventually relocated to Ghana where he died at the age 95

Marcus Garvey was charged with mail fraud and was deported. He died in London at the age of 52. Marcus had been surrounded by agents to set him up after purchasing his first ship for The Black Star Line.

In August of 1920 the 19th Amendment was ratified giving women the right to vote.

Credits Roll as we quote stupid things politicians say

"These kids have come and they have done very,very well. They aren't just Hispanics they are also Asian and Pacific Islanders. In many cases they are more American than most Americans, because they have done well in school"

Joe Biden, 2020

"Maxine Waters is leading, Maxine, she's a real beauty, a seriously low I.Q.person, seriously"

President Donald Trump, 2018

"People who say there's no federal law against lynching are not telling the truth"

Rand Paul, 2020

BONUS

John F. Kennedy: Breaking 1877

A bullet leaves the body of Lee Harvey Oswald and travels back into the gun of Jack Ruby. Jack Ruby steps outside and he checks to make sure his gun is on him. Lee Harvey Oswald goes back into his jail cell. Lee sits in his cell thinking about the death of John F. Kennedy, possibly the greatest president in American history. The guards come and get Lee Harvey Oswald out of his cell. They unbook him and he heads outside of the jail. They get back into the police car and drive away. The detectives let Lee Harvey Oswald out of the car and remove his handcuffs. His rights are unread and he goes back into hiding. Lee Harvey Oswald heads back up to the 6th floor of the school book depository.

Multiple bullets head back into multiple rifles. One bullet leaves the leg of Governor Connolly, goes through the neck of John F. Kennedy and heads back into the rifle of Lee Harvey Oswald.(Another bullet exits the head of John F. Kennedy) Lee Harvey lowers his rifle and backs out of the book depository. John F. Kennedy sits up and starts waving to onlookers in Dallas. President Kennedy gives a speech and him and his wife head back onto Air Force

One.

Air Force One lands back in D.C. and John F. Kennedy and his staff exits. Kennedy heads back into the The White House and has a conversation on the phone with his brother Bobby.

Bobby Kennedy: I want you know that I am so proud of you brother. Be careful, you pissed off some pretty powerful people.

John F. Kennedy: I will not bow down to any secret society, I will do what is right.

Bobby Kennedy: Hey, I will see you after Dallas. Have a good time.

John F. Kennedy:

The Alabama National Guard was required for the entry of two clearly qualified students to enter the University of Alabama. We can no longer say that we are a democracy for everyone except Negroes. We do not ask for white people only, when we send soldiers to Vietnam or West Berlin. I will be asking Congress to create legislation that will allow black Americans to be able access public facilities which to me seems like the most basic of rights. We can't do it all through legislation but Americans will also have to take responsibility in their household. American Citizens of every color should be able to go to public school anywhere they wish to and any American Citizen should be able to access things such as hotels and restaurants which seem to me like the most elementary of rights. The heart of the question is should all Americans have equal rights and equal opportunities? If they cannot enjoy the same freedom that all of us want for ourselves then who among us would want to stand in their place? There must be a way for citizens to redress the wrongs that are done to them and if we don't provide that then their only option is to take to the streets.

(John F. Kennedy heads into his office to address his staff before giving his address on Civil Rights)

Lyndon B. Johnson: I think you might be moving too fast boss. You're going to lose the support of a lot of southern white Democrats.

John F. Kennedy: We can no longer be a nation of hypocrites. We have held on to this peculiar system of ours long enough. I have no choice but to follow suit of recent federal court rulings and to ask congress to create a new Civil Rights Act.

Secretary: I agree in spirit, but there is a long standing unwritten agreement that in America it must be forever white over black.

John F. Kennedy: I am well aware of the so called compromise of 1877. I cannot agree with it. That election is long over and these citizens, who built this country should not be locked out of the country they built. If any staff is not with me and you want to walk away, I fully understand.

Lyndon B. Johnson: We should take our time and slowly move things along but that trouble maker Dr. Martin Luther King Jr. keeps aggressively pushing for legislation that includes voting with civil rights. I get it, the 15th Amendment should allow the Negroes to vote in theory but we can't just force that on Americans.

John F. Kennedy: It's hard to say that if I was Rev. Dr. Martin Luther King Jr. that I wouldn't want the same thing.

Lyndon B. Johnson: You sound like Bobby now boss.

John F. Kennedy: Are you ready to create a real democracy?

[African-Americans at this point had lived through about 250 years of slavery, followed by 9 years of freedom and then 90 years of mob rule, before finally getting the same rights on paper as white citizens]

INTO OBLIVION

E.J. Wade

I have come to notice that Democrats and Republicans alike have no respect for the United States Constitution. After all, they all but destroyed it once it was amended to include rights for Foundational Black Americans. Republicans only mention the constitution when they want to use the 2nd Amendment. Democrats only use the 1st Amendment unless we are talking about Immigration, then they will "whip out" the 14th Amendment.

What is the United States Constitution? The United States Constitution is what they call a primary source of law. You have The Constitution, case law, statutes and ordinances and administrative law. Not only is the constitution a primary source of law but it is the primary source of law that all other laws must be in line with. The United States Constitution is made up of 7 articles.

Article **one** gives legislative power to congress. Congress is made up of a Senate and a House of Representatives. That is why when you first see a bill introduced, it will have an H.R. or an S to show you where the bill originated. Congress can write a bill, but they cannot sign their own bills into law. That is why they have these long battles every 4 years to elect a President.

Article **two** grants executive power to the President of the United States. This guy or lady (now) gets their own branch of government called the Executive Branch. They also determine much of administrative law as well, when the EPA is slow to respond to residents being poisoned by their own elected officials in Flint, Michigan, that is usually because the President did not order them to take effective enough action. The funny part about Administrative Law is they are given powers by congress but operate under the executive branch.

Article **three** gives power to the judicial branch or the Supreme Court and other Federal Courts. The job of the Federal Courts is to interpret law but once an Appellate court publishes its opinion it becomes the law. For example, The Dred Scott decision. The evil Supreme Court decision that started so much conflict had to be defeated by a constitutional Amendment.

Article **four** deals with full faith and credit. In quick dummy terms, my driver's license in Florida is good while traveling to New York. Also if you kill someone in New York and run to Florida, New York can order that you be shipped back up to New York. This article, as boring as it looks will cause great controversy for returning runaway enslaved humans in America.

Article **five,** two-thirds of both houses can amend the constitution and then the amendments must be ratified by three-fourths of all states. Traitor states that committed treason against America had to agree to ratify the 14th Amendment in order to be fully restored after the Civil

War.

Article **six**, Federal law is supreme law. In other words, the 90 years after the 14th Amendment was passed, for every year the 14th Amendments rights were ignored, the descendants of slavery and victims of Jim Crow and their descendants should be compensated for the total disregard of federal law.

Article **seven:** Nine of the thirteen colonies were needed to adopt the constitution. Article 7 ties all of the states together. Article seven is the reason President Lincoln can determine the traitors who committed treason had no rights to leave. They could leave as individual traitors but had no rights to take the state with them. In other words, you can leave, but leave the keys to my house!

Amendments to the Constitution

The First 10 Amendments are the Bill of Rights

Amendment 1: Freedom of religion, freedom of speech, freedom of press, freedom of assembly and freedom to petition the government. What do they mean by freedom to petition the government? If we have a grievance we can petition the government to correct it. No state may make a law saying we cannot petition the government.

Amendment 2: A well-regulated militia being necessary to the security of a free state. The right of the people to keep and bear arms shall not be infringed.

Amendment 3: No citizen can be forced to provide lodging for soldiers in their homes.

Amendment 4: The fourth Amendment prevents the

government (including police) from searching or seizing the homes, belongings, or bodies of citizens without probable cause (not to be confused with being briefly detained for reasonable suspicion) or a warrant.

Amendment 5: The right to grand jury indictment for felony offenses in federal court, the restriction on double jeopardy, protection against forced self-incrimination, the guarantee of due process of law and the prevention of government taking private property for public use without proper compensation.

Amendment 6: The right to a speedy and public trial

Amendment 7: The right to a jury trial for property over 20 dollars.

Amendment 8: Protects from excessive bail or cruel and unusual punishment from the federal government.

Amendment 9: Just because a particular right is not listed in the constitution does not mean a person does not have that right.

Amendment 10: Federalism in a nutshell. What the federal government controls, it controls it absolutely but what the federal government does not control can be controlled by the states or the people.

Reconstruction Amendments

Amendment 13: Abolishes the institution of slavery. *

Except as punishment for a crime where the party shall have been duly convicted. The 13th Amendment ended slavery for many people but to circumvent the 13th

Amendment states started making everything a crime. It was a crime to walk around without a permission slip from a white person is some areas of the U.S.

Amendment 14: All persons born or naturalized in the United States and subject to its jurisdiction are citizens of the United States and the states they reside in. No state shall make or enforce any law which abridges the privileges or immunities of citizens of the United States; nor shall any state deprive any person life, liberty, or property without due process of law; nor deny any person within its jurisdiction equal protection of the laws.

No constitutional Amendment has been violated more than the 14th Amendment. From 1877 until 1965 officially and even up until today unofficially, states have repeatedly violated the 14th Amendment. (Read *The Crow Code 1877*)

Section 3 of the 14th Amendment also prevents traitors who committed treason (confederates) from walking back into government like the treason never happened. Congress would have to agree by two-thirds vote to allow them to return to a government position.

Amendment 15: guarantees the right to vote (for men), meaning white men already had it and the amendment stops discrimination in voting based on race but not gender.

Amendment 19: Gives women the right to vote.

There are a total of 27 Amendments to the U.S. Constitution.

To Black Americans, who continue to argue about which of these two unconstitutional parties should get our support, be careful not to become a mini colonizer or servant of evil. The entire time our ancestors were being blown to pieces for trying to vote, they were still voting for the Republican Party. The party of Lincoln died in 1877 and they became largely silent while over 4,000 Foundational Black Americans were lynched.

The blatant disrespect for black lives started in 1619 of course but the disrespect for our citizenship started in 1877. Today you can witness the white supremacist riding around with Nazi flags and Confederate flags. Two groups who attempted to destroy America. A lot of these so called patriots never really cared about America in the first place. They cared about status. They cared about a new system that took them from peasant status to "Gods over African people due to the invention of gun powder, by the Asians".

Today, we have thought leaders, who are not capable of thinking, who have been chosen by the dominate society. I am calling on all Foundational Black Americans to abandon partisan politics and stick to the constitution. We have to put an end to this dishonest conversation with dishonest language. We built America, enslaved Africans built America and then got locked out of the country we built. The large buildings that populate the downtown skyline represent a hidden white economy. Year after year, young whites graduate from college and gain access to jobs through a referral system. A network that African-Americans can't access and here we are trying to compete with it. Your application won't even be viewed, you have already lost. This is why we need a black wealth apparatus.

We keep trying to survive with "as long as I get mine" culture. This does not work…Black men have been locked out of every private sector job except trucking.

The Black Wealth Apparatus takes the institution building power of Booker T. Washington and creates black owned businesses instead of schools. Call on every Foundational Black American to pay 1.00 per month and call on white allies, (The real white allies) to donate to a real Black Wealth Apparatus.

The blind spot that Booker T. Washington had was enormous. What he didn't understand was even with powerful institutions, without 1st class citizenship you could lose it all in the blink of an eye. According to the report by George Edmund Haynes there were attacks in the following cities during the Red Summer:

Bedford County, Tennessee

Blakeley, Georgia

Pace, Florida

Memphis, Tennessee

Morgan County, West Virginia

Jenkins County, Georgia

Sylvester, Georgia

Millen, Georgia two times

Pickens, Mississippi

Charleston, South Carolina

El Dorado, Arkansas

New London, Connecticut

Annapolis, Maryland

Macon, Mississippi

Bisbee, Arizona

Scranton, Pennsylvania

Dublin, Georgia

Philadelphia, Pennsylvania two times

Coatesville, Pennsylvania

Tuscaloosa, Alabama

Longview, Texas

Baltimore, Maryland

Louise, Mississippi

Port Arthur, Texas

Washington, D.C.

New York, New York two times

Norfolk, Virginia

New Orleans, Louisiana

Darby, Pennsylvania

Hobson City, Alabama

Chicago, Illinois

New Berry, South Carolina

Bloomington, Illinois

Syracuse, New York

Whatley Alabama

Lincoln Arkansas

Hattiesburg, Mississippi

Texarkana, Texas

Austin, Texas

Ocmulgee, Georgia

Knoxville, Tennessee

Bogalusa, Louisiana

Clarksdale, Mississippi

Omaha, Nebraska

Montgomery, Alabama

Elaine, Arkansas

Baltimore, Maryland

Corbin Kentucky

Macon Georgia

Magnolia, Arkansas

Wilmington, Delaware

Booker T. Washington, in all of his brilliance could not

see the blind spot. Descendants of Slavery have no choice but to seek 1st class citizenship status. Without it, it allows people to repeatedly destroy what we build. Today you have Immigrants who get right off of the boat, or just make it over the boarder than they get a "model minority comparison" yet the Japanese got reparations for 4 years of internment. White America have burned down so many black neighborhoods and businesses that you could fill a dictionary sized book on all of the areas they burned down. Ask an Immigrant from anywhere to count on one hand the amount of towns they built that were destroyed. (In America)There are no model minorities, you either got what you built burned down or you didn't. There are no groups in America whose history can compare to ours. There are no situations in the United States that can compare to ours. If a white liberal comes to my door to talk to me about climate change, I say I need to change my climate first. When they reply, "but we are talking about the entire planet", my response is well you better get started with ending white supremacy today so that we can help you with the ice caps tomorrow!

It is the erasure of Foundational Black Americans that allow anybody and everybody to attach themselves to our struggle in order to benefit. Drop all of the dishonest language. "People of Color" did not get lynched, we did. When Italians got lynched in New Orleans in 1891, not only did America put a quick stop to it, but they created a holiday known as Columbus Day. You couldn't find another name for an American holiday other than one named after a salve trader? "Black and Brown" people did not get enslaved, we did. As a matter of fact, when you fill out an application, there is no such thing as brown people. If you check white on an application, that makes you white. We are an accepting people, capable of getting along with all groups. We shall show respect for all groups, but never at the cost of harming ourselves or allowing disrespect to ourselves.

[In Miami Florida, a young lady was refused service at a Taco Bell by a Latino Immigrant. She threatened to call the police. She told the young lady she was in Hiahleah. In other words, this lady could barely speak English but did not want to serve a black woman and did not think that black woman had the right to be there. How are you in our country and you don't even understand rights?]

Foundational Black Americans are supposed to get our own unique protected status just like Native Americans did. We have allowed people to dance around this issue to the point to where they think we are asking for something special when we say America must fix what it destroyed. The irony of some of the groups that came to America after us is that they ran from a country where many of them look like the majority yet they tell us our history is not valid as we fight in a country where the majority does not look like us. Now people want to label us xenophobic, for refusing to allow people to come to the country we built and join in with the oppressor class as so many have done before. After fighting for centuries in America for citizenship, we have elites who want to do away with borders and citizenship because now their wealth solidifies their citizenship. They are also causing a brain drain where many talented and educated people can stay where they are and fight for democracy at home.

We can never be anti-American, America is an idea. It is some of the people who exist within America that have caused us problems. We can never be anti- government, the government belongs to the people and the constitution lays out our inalienable rights given by our creator. Be careful with who you allow to wear the history of Ida B. Wells.

Our great ancestor, who I owe a great deal of respect to, never intended on the two genders to be separated. Ida B. Wells's idea of what we now call feminism was all about no limitations on women. She also believed that there should be no limitations on black men. Ida B. Wells was against any form of violence against women. She was also against any form of violence against black men. This was a married woman, with a family, and love and respect for her husband and sons but was bold enough to name one of her daughters Ida B. Wells- Barnett Jr. Her intersectionality meant freedom for all, it did not mean to allow others to hijack the black struggle and suffering for their own gain.

As I close out. Allow me to touch on the times we are living in. In 2017 the FBI reported the infiltration into law enforcement agencies by white extremist. Now we face a battle where some members of law enforcement have chosen to act outside of the "color of law". The white supremacist in America pretend to back these crooked individuals because brave people like Ida B. Wells put an end to mob rule. If the government is the people's government then we don't have to deal with crooked law enforcement. If that person is acting outside of the color of law at that point he or she is no longer law enforcement acting in an official capacity. Either they should be held accountable or the mayor and police chief should be held accountable. I say this not in hatred for police but to protect the police as well as citizens.

A message to the black boule and the "talented-tenth", your time is up. You will never speak for the black grassroots again. You don't have the muscle and you don't have the backbone. We will not allow you to remove the contributions of Ida B. Wells from history. Black men and black women are here to protect each other. We cover the 12 and our women cover our 6.(make no mistake about it on her side she covers the 12 and we cover her 6, that's what I call equality) You will never shut the black grassroots up again. You will never tell us what our agenda is and what we should vote for. You will never disrespect or remove the name of Ida B. Wells-Barnett again.

I leave you as a reader with 3 missions. (History will tell if we accomplish this or not)

1. Move to a fully constitutional government at all levels, including law enforcement.(move away from partisan politics, they cause most of our issues)

2. Create a black wealth apparatus

3. Let's bring Ida B. Wells-Barnett to the big screen using this story. The most accurate telling of her life ever written and let's make sure a Black woman who is a descendant of American Slavery plays the role of Ida B. Wells in her movie. Not in disrespect of anyone, but because she is our ancestor. We have been the ones here fighting against tyranny for now over 400 years. It is time we get some respect!

Nothing Left

The Free Will Rise Again

E.J. Wade

In loving memory:

Addie Mae Collins

Cynthia Wesley

Carole Robertson

Carol Denise McNair

IDA B. WELLS.

LINEAGE, HISTORY, PRIDE, CULTURE

Made in the USA
Las Vegas, NV
04 February 2021

17177017R00135